golf
unplugged

golf
unplugged

• • • • jim apfelbaum • • • •

tatra press

TATRA
PRESS

Contact: Tatra Press LLC, 292 Spook Rock Road, Suffern, NY 10901.
tatrapress@hotmail.com tel/fax 845.357.4843

Text composed by Stephanie Bart-Horvath
Printed in the United States.
Book design by Stephanie Bart-Horvath
U.S. Library of Congress Control Number: 2007926603

ISBN: 0-9776142-2-0
ISBN 13: 978-0-9776142-2-6

To a feature pairing: David White, Mike Brown, Jack Marr and Eddy Davis for continued support and club selection. And in fond memory of Joe Balander who I hope won't mind. Golf, he said, is a game of "feel, instinct and resolve."

people are talking about golf unplugged...

Here is writing that's subtle, thoroughly self-effacing and informative. ...a very thoughtful read.
    —Bradley Klein, *GolfWeek*

Nothing short of delightful.
    —Ben Wright, *author of Good Bounces & Bad Lies*

"Mr. _____ respectfully asks that you not contact him again."
    —Name withheld

"Does he play our clubs?"
    —B.H., Fort Worth

"The finest book of its type I've ever received."
    —G.P., Orlando

Returned mail: Host unknown (Name server: host not found)
    —Daemon Mailer

With Hagen at Sandwich.

• • • • • c o n t e n t s • • • • •

A smiling George Seaholm demonstrates
proper club breaking technique.

*Q: We're almost at the end of this tape but I want to know
if you have any concerns for the future of the game?*

*A: The future of the game? The future of the game rests
on one thing. More public courses and cheaper golf. So
that people that work in factories and work elsewhere they
can go out and enjoy a round of golf, not give up their
whole salary to play one round of golf. All equipment has
got to be cheaper. It's too expensive now.*

—Gene Sarazen, interviewed by Alice M. Kendrick, February 8, 1991

• • • • introduction • • • •

Please be seated. We've got a lot of material to cover. Welcome to
a source of holistic golf edification. Wait! Come back! Let me
explain. *Golf Unplugged* is, first, an awareness born of a sense of unease.
It wasn't the attempts to co-opt the game to sell cars, *tschotchkes*, or get
a cheap laugh in the comics that chapped me. Those ruggedly hand-
some models grasping a club as if it might bite? I'm glad they can find
work. No, what finally did it was a club lock for golf bags, with an
alarm no less. *What* is going on? Portable indoor-outdoor ball flight
monitors, handheld GPS range-finders, pockets *designed* for cell
phones, computerized golf instruction, bag alarms, who needs it?

This is a game that sprung from the well of Man's imagination. Other
than the lawn mower, which sportswriter Waxo Green believed was
the game's greatest invention, arguably the rest of it is flapdoodle.
Feel, instinct and resolve cannot be purchased, downloaded, patented
or up-linked. A top teaching pro told me he tries to learn something
new about golf everyday. That's what I'm talking about. That's 'deh,'

inner sincerity, basically bringing to the table a good attitude and an open mind. Wait! Come back! That's the end of the spiritual quest. Clubs, balls, tees, a bag, maybe a glove, the flag, occasionally a rake, and at the start and finish of the round, your opponent's hand. These are all that need be handheld. One's sensitivities and consideration for others and the course are all that need be plugged in.

Golf is best enjoyed on hind legs and, as Harry Vardon suggested, in comparative silence. There are sounds worth savoring. Gary Player has written that he found comforting the click of persimmon, the clatter of cleat on pavement, the white noise on a true links. The sound a cart makes in backing up is not comforting.

"I believe that what we have today in the game is the best that has survived," suggested Howard Whitney, a USGA president. That was in 1922. It's true today. Buffeted by technology golf better hold on tight. We seem to have forgotten that less is more.

Golf Unplugged is the legendary Old Tom Morris observed "one cold, frosty morning" long ago by a bystander who believed he was witnessing "a man on the beach trying hard to drown himself." It was only Old Tom, W.W. Tulloch wrote, "breaking the ice to enjoy his usual morning dip in the sea, for he made a practice of bathing all year round, not withstanding the state of the atmosphere."

Golf Unplugged is the spirit of George Seaholm. A city champion in the early '50s, George once won the right to caddie for Ben Hogan during an exhibition. The Hawk paid the lad $5 when 65 cents was a decent wage. George played a lot of golf at The Municipal in Austin, as it was then known. He was, looking back with pride and a broad smile, a "muny hooter," the golf equivalent of a gym rat. George caddied from age 11 to 19. Later, he arranged his hours with the phone company to allow him to play nearly every day, which he did for probably 40 years. I defer to him for the definitive word on club-breaking. "I will never forget," he said. "The ladies had an outing and invited all the men and everything. And this lady—she takes this club and she's going to break it over her knee—and she held it up, and it comes down and hits her knee. Man! She had a big knot. When you break a club, you've got to hold it against your knee, and then pull *up*."

The two genial codgers on page 10 were regulars at another venerable public course, Buncombe County in Asheville, North Carolina. There was an old hospital on that hill, they pointed out as we climbed one fairway. Tuberculosis patients who could make it up were deemed cured; many tragically failed the primitive test. The finishing hole at Buncombe is sublime. A greenside bunker is somehow shielded from the tee…on a steep downhill par-three! A sly and unplugged architectural sleight of hand by Donald Ross. These gentlemen were wonderful to me. All we shared was a love of the game.

Since there's a law that golf books must include tips, impress your friends and **Master the Fundamentals.**

These and the other tales explore golf's unplugged terrain, peeking into inviting historical nooks and crannies. The fuss over the ancient stymie, the early presidential devotion to golf—damn the political torpedoes! -- letters exchanged among old friends—the hope is that they will kindle an urge to kick back and occasionally pull the plug. If these tales inspire an interest in golf beyond the confines of the scorecard, obviously I'd be delighted. What do I know about it? Not much. But I'm learning, hopefully something new every day.

Hogan's office lovingly recreated.

one

• • • • the sixth lesson • • • •

Pete kept a small and neat, if slightly seedy, basement apartment in a forlorn nook of Raleigh. The worn carpet smelled of past floods. The light was awful, the furnishings spartan. His health was not much better than his surroundings but the sparkle in his eyes was bright. Jolly and voluble despite his advanced age and declining health, next to him I felt dull, responsible. His disposition remained so supremely sunny, and he was so passionate about his research that time with him always passed quickly. No writer, Pete nevertheless understood the importance of piecing together threads. Answering basic questions.

His beat was the prolific Scottish emigrant course architect Donald Ross. Pete wanted to know how Ross's operation worked. Literally hundreds of courses bear his imprimatur, many of them justly revered. Some were hands-on, others Ross never laid eyes on. Establishing the pedigree of a Ross course has been dicey business. Until Pete's efforts, Ross courses were as glibly referenced as George Washington's sleeping arrangements. Pete enjoyed working the puzzle. After his heart finally succumbed, now over a decade ago, *Golfweek's* Bradley Klein picked up the trail. He put Pete's digging to good use. The result was the award-winning, *Discovering Donald Ross*.

"This book would not have been possible without years of prior work by the late W. Pete Jones of Raleigh, North Carolina," Klein acknowledged. "He poured his soul into accumulating, sorting, and cataloging many thousands of letters, files, maps, and notes generated during the course of Donald Ross's life." True enough. Pete sought to connect the dots. He spoke of previously unheralded Ross subordinates like old friends. Pete would be delighted to know he helped foster a deeper appreciation of Ross's Shaker-like genius. The book is a fitting tribute to both men. A row of neatly arranged boxes lines a shelf in the Tuft's Archive in Pinehurst, North Carolina, the site of Ross's epic achievement, further testament to Pete's effort.

He gave me several treasured reference books along with one other bequest, an odd little story. Pete said it came from a most reliable source, as it happens at a cocktail party. The following morning Pete called the source. There were a couple of things about the yarn he wanted to get straight. Much to his surprise the acquaintance not only did not want to talk about it, he denied ever saying it. Several times, before and after Pete's death, I attempted to verify the story by contacting the source. Nada.

Of course I'm biased but Pete had nothing to gain by inventing the tale. It is, I admit, a remarkable assertion. Pete said that there was a missing lesson to Hogan's great work: *Five Lessons: The Modern Fundamentals of Golf*, and he shared it with me.

Written with the late Herbert Wind and enhanced by Anthony Ravielli's illustrations, *Five Lessons* remains a classic. The omission, goes the story, surfaced during a Carnoustie practice round prior to the 1953 British Open. Hogan blamed its exclusion on pressures to complete the manuscript.

Five Lessons was published in 1957, four years after Hogan's triumph at Carnoustie. This was not an e-book to be sure, but one would assume that even in the fifties four years would have afforded sufficient time, even for an avowed perfectionist, to make the inevitable corrections, let alone cover an essential tenet. I never asked Wind (who was not the original source), and now it's too late. I'm not suggesting that Hogan overlooked or forgot it. That's incomprehensible. If Ben Hogan thought the instruction worthy of inclusion it would've been there. There is, however, another possibility. Could the tip have been deliberately omitted?

We call Jody Vasquez to the stand. Vasquez for a time shagged balls for Hogan at Shady Oaks, an honor not lost on the then-Fort Worth teenager and high school golfer. In a delightful memoir, *Afternoons with Mr. Hogan*, Vasquez recalls their time together with commendable restraint. Vasquez is now himself a member at Colonial Country Club where Hogan's presence remains omnipresent.

The former shag boy writes about a conversation regarding the illustrious Hogan Secret, a source of eternal fascination. Hogan devotees will find Vasquez's recollections compelling as will, frankly, anyone inquisitive about the golf swing. The apprentice was dutiful, deferential, inquisitive but not cloying in the reclusive golfer's presence. He showed up, kept up and shut up. Hogan took a shine to him.

Over time, Vasquez wrestled with his conscience reluctant to betray a confidence. After all these years, though, he believes that Hogan meant for him to share the gist of that momentous conversation, which is detailed in his book.

The aspiring golfer one day asked Hogan why something as important as The Secret was excluded from *Five Lessons*. The question exasperated Hogan. He placed "his hands on his hips and said, "I'm not telling them this!" Vasquez recalled. Well, then. Maybe Ben didn't forget Pete's sixth lesson at all, or for that matter, the seventh and eighth lessons, whatever those may have been. No, maybe the man who no less than Jack Nicklaus has said hit more good shots and fewer bad shots than anyone in history chose not to include it. Maybe he felt some things were best left to the golfer to suss out for himself, another answer, as he famously said, for each golfer to dig from the dirt.

Surely, there can be no objection to characterizing Hogan as reserved in his dealings with the outside world, especially when it came to the golf swing. This reticence would naturally include his fellow competitors, the likely 'them' in his retort. (As Vasquez notes, Hogan was still competing when *Five Lessons* was first published, so his reluctance to open the vault to his opposition is certainly reasonable.)

About Pete's story—look, who knows? The suggestion that Hogan chose to conceal it is at least plausible. Perhaps he never had any intention of including it. Or, there may have been publishing glitches that prevented his doing so. Maybe he did just say (albeit more colorfully): 'Let 'em figure it out on their own.' Maybe Hogan, who did not teach, had had enough of translating instruction for the lazy golfing masses, a realization certainly familiar to lesser champions. A walk through the discount stacks will attest to the genre's challenge. Only those who have sat down to write instruction can fully appreciate the difficulty. As articulate as any golfer in history, Bob Jones observed that it was far easier to demonstrate a proper swing than to describe it.

the curse of the book deal. . . .

The accomplished golfer faces a further complication. A curse seems to settle upon those who rush their own secrets into print. Tiger's dominance, and his own formulaic instruction book, undoubtedly has put a dent in the market (Who else is there?).

Still, the thirst for quick and painless relief among mortal golfers remains unquenched. An unwelcome consequence, the win-a-major, write-a-book assembly line has repeatedly had a debilitating effect on numerous champions. It is as if the very act of stopping to consider the methods that made them champions has somehow imperiled their fate.

Here's how the curse works. Having won a big one, the newly-heralded pro is swayed from his or her own personal righteous (swing) path. As if on cue, fortunes invariably sour soon after (or even by) publication. It's long been known in top teaching circles that winning a major championship introduces a dangerous double-edged luxury. Free from the specter of worrying over his schedule, or the yoke of making cuts, our champion is finally free to "work" on his game, refine away the kinks and, "take it to the next level." The winner of the U.S. Open automatically enjoys a five-year pass to the other major championships, and a 10-year exemption as a past champion. An LPGA win is good for a three-year exemption. The guarantees provide stability and confidence to a delicate psyche in a fiercely competitive environment. With victory come temptations, change and a karmic crossroads.

With the best of intentions, the golfer risks fixing things that aren't broken, messing with the mojo that was, after all, good enough to win in the first place. Winning presents many opportunities too good to pass up. There will be offers to change clubs. Lucrative international corporate outings materialize. Who can blame the newly crowned winner for getting *some*? The biggest threat becomes maintaining balance and focus. The game doesn't become harder but other things do, and his game often suffers as a result. Our champion becomes increasingly uncomfortable with the demands on his time, heightened expectations and pressures, and after toiling in obscurity in a lonely sport for so long, the attention. It becomes less fun. The next big thing or the current man-of-the-moment becomes a remember-when, then a where-has-he-been to a whatever-happened-to. It may be a short but still lucrative ride. With sound investment advice and a long view his family and several succeeding generations may be provided for, but the ride, without sustained good play, will soon come to an end. A long and distinguished list of players have learned that maintaining success is much harder than breaking the ice.

The slide may be gradual or precipitous.

It would be absurd to view winning as a hardship; that is, after all, the objective. But there are clear and present dangers. A second noteworthy, if smaller, list would include those who have rebounded in time to reestablish their moorings, to become stronger and wiser as golfers and as individuals. That pro golfers are routinely blindsided by the trappings of success—as so often happens with entrepreneurs or inventors—is just another one of those similarities between sport and life. As with the game they play, their ability to adjust ultimately determines success.

Two final points. Translating a motion as complex as the golf swing (which one instructor likens to a swimming fish) in print is absolute drudgery, if not impossible. How does one convey feel in words? Lack of commitment from the author may also be shared, if not exceeded, by indifference on the part of the reader. Those with a life outside the game, a family, a job, are bound to glaze over trying to relate to the single-minded devotion of the professional golfer. And, *vice versa*. Lord knows, to say nothing of the disparity of commitment between the two, technical positions in the swing that pros attain would put many recreational golfers in traction. Aside from their relative delusions, the pro and the duffer have almost nothing in common.

Regrettably, the hope of a better game feeds a powerful delusion, if successful business model. Golf has proven remarkably resilient, largely impervious to man's best efforts. Recreational golfers labor under the illusion that they can improve without commitment. The equipment industry does its best to accommodate them.

Despite strides in teaching and the marvels of technology, the masses remain the equivalent of barefoot and pregnant. More sophisticated aids, learning materials and techniques—more magazines, more drills, more technology, more outlandish claims, More! More! More!—have made nary a statistical dent in our collective ability to improve.

It must be said. Numerous champions have succeeded without any formal instruction whatsoever. They merely tagged along, watching, absorbing the game and its subtleties. This was most famously the case with the toddler Bobby Jones, who picked up the game by osmosis. Golf, then, emerges as yet another language that comes much more easily to the young.

An intriguing question: Can the game be learned by reading a book, watching a video, or, once upon a time, even by listening to a record? There is scant evidence in support. We know that Greg Norman's mother purchased two Jack Nicklaus books for her 16-year old son, *Golf My Way* and *My 55 Ways to Lower Your Golf Score*, and that Greg promptly dropped his handicap from 27 to 2 in two years. But, sadly, that must say more about young Greg's prodigious talents and dedication. Nick Price, the personable PGA and British Open champion, growing up in Rhodesia, received his first instruction listening at 33 1/3 *Mircrogrooves* to the stilted conversation between Chris Schenkel and Arnold Palmer. The two-record set, *Arnold Palmer's Personal Golf Instruction* (From Driver thru Putter), included a 24-page instructional booklet "with detailed photographs showing each important step—corresponding to ARNOLD PALMER'S recorded lessons.".... For good reason, Arnold does not sing on the recording, which Jimmy Demaret does quite capably on his own boxed-set in pitching tempo to an earlier generation. We have to take Nick's word about how much help the record provided. "Like most kids," he wrote in his own book on playing the game, "I was more impressed with the sound of the club hitting the ball than with any of the instruction." Oh, well. The novel attempt remains a cherished collectible for golf audiophiles. At the risk of a pun, the information imparted is probably sound. Two other champions who turned out of necessity to golf books are Walter Travis and Larry Nelson. Nelson devoured *Five Lessons* but crediting the book would, it seems, unfairly accentuate its impact against his own heart and determination, not to mention his talent.

the curse of the equipment deal. . . .

"[Club company X] and I have an understanding," the newly-crowned PGA Champion shared with the media a few months after his historic win. He was responding to a question regarding his new club contract. His ability to do so with a straight face only again demonstrates the touring pro's highly developed aversion to irony. Wasn't he worried about switching clubs, that notorious harbinger to disaster? After his big win the inevitable offers appeared. He jumped when the right one came along. Why the pros get the big money is hard to fathom. Do recreational golfers really buy what the touring pros are paid to play? Smarter marketing minds must be able to make a compelling case or the endorsement dollars wouldn't flow. A demographic of whom it's said likes to read the ads, golfers must realize that the clubs and balls always work better for Tiger, Phil, Ernie, etc., never mind for the largely anonymous though still very good golfers who struggle to keep their tour card than they ever will for them. To think otherwise would be to believe that expensive paints and brushes are all that's needed to assure a masterpiece.

No, he said, he wasn't concerned about switching clubs. The champion then made a surprising admission. The first models of the clubs he was now playing, he confessed, resembled "an Earth shoe at the end of a shaft." It was a good line and we laughed. (He was talking about the earliest Callaway woods.) It may not have been a promising start to a long-term relationship but it wasn't about that, despite his candor. It was about The Money. The *understanding* he referred to was an offer too good to refuse.

To no one's surprise, perhaps even his own, his game subsequently fell off. There may have been absolutely nothing wrong with the new clubs but they were different. For the pros laboring so long to achieve control in all aspects of their golf, different is always suspect. The offers declined as his struggles compounded. So did his newfound celebrity and, we can assume to his quiet relief, flattering though it may have been, the fuss. He eventually went back to his old familiar irons. No longer a marquee player nor, if he ever was, much of a draw, the endorsement window closed. It's an old story and not just in golf, or even in sports. It is the rare athlete who can back away from his first visit to victory's smorgasbord. Would any of us be so pompous to think we would handle it any differently? The lesson, repeatedly overlooked, is that when the *brega*, the business, is first taken care of, the money invariably follows. The truly exceptional athletes, survivors and masters on so many levels, seem to grasp this or at least heed the warnings and advice of wise counsel.

the alleged sixth lesson. . . .

In the second of his five lessons, Hogan addresses stance, posture and footwork. Like so much else in golf, the alleged missing lesson is more easily demonstrated than described, easy to do but hard to accomplish. Pete said he got it from a writer/broadcaster close (enough) to Hogan who accompanied him to Scotland for the '53 Open. The tale's provenance may be debatable. The ingenuity and efficacy of the tip, suggests the five handicap, are sound.

A wide angled view of any driving range will confirm the importance of balance. Those who finish their swing resembling the opening of a somersault bear witness to problems from the ground up. The pros display impeccable stability. This firm foundation is the basis of the alleged missing lesson, and the principle is easily demonstrated.

Stand casually. Were someone to lightly push you backwards in the chest, you would lose your footing. Now stand erect, feet together, weight evenly distributed. Assume your golf stance, this time by moving only the back leg into position to the proper width of the stance. That's it. That's the lesson. The hard part is not establishing the position but in remaining there by keeping the right foot planted. The urge to shuffle and slightly adjust the feet is overwhelming. For the sake of discussion, resist it. Now, were someone to try and push you back you barely budge. You're grounded. As those who study his swing know, Hogan also liked to turn the toe of his front foot slightly out, which in no way imperils the desired stability.

A former student of legendary Texas teacher Harvey Penick's, now up in years though still an exceptional ball striker, comes very close to enacting this procedure to the letter. He told me that Harvey advocated something very similar to the alleged tip. Another Penick acolyte confirms this. This man, a life member of the PGA of America, told me that Harvey did indeed like his students to address the ball with both feet together and then move the back foot into position. Try it. It's very hard to leave the feet still. The urge to waggle or lift is neigh irresistible, but there's no mistaking the centering. The legs feel more secure and surely this must promote good balance. As Hogan elaborated: "The proper stance and posture enable a golfer to be perfectly balanced and poised throughout the swing. Only then will his legs, arms, and body be able to carry out their interrelated assignments correctly."

For corroboration a superlative snapshot of Hogan's swing, circa 1964, was consulted. On an old *Shell's Wonderful World of Golf* show, riveting despite the travelogue kitsch, Hogan and Sam Snead played a very wet and very long Houston Country Club. Thunder periodically booms in the background. Delays plagued the taping. The weather and television's exigencies made it slow going, not to mention a soggy Robert Trent Jones, Sr. 7,000-yard golf course played in full bore Houston humidity. They were up to it. "That's as well as I think I've ever seen Ben play," Snead marveled afterwards. Host Gene Sarazen gushed that it was the finest round he'd ever seen. Hogan shot 69, three-under par, despite taking forever over his putts. A fan told Red Smith, who wrote a column about the match, that watching the titans was right up there with "the War Admiral-Seabiscuit match race,

Graziano-Zale, and Don Larsen's perfect game."

Hogan starts his set-up differently on the tape than the move Pete described. He begins by placing his right foot in position, then brings in his left foot, steps it out slightly, where it stays, does the same with his right foot, takes a couple of waggles, then pulls the trigger. It's not the precise move that Pete described. There's certainly nothing remotely mechanical about it. A creamy quality suffuses everything Hogan does with a club in his hands, set-up included. Anyone troubled by movement in their lower body while putting will also find Pete's recollection useful and much easier to settle into than for the full swing. Maybe Hogan amended the sixth lesson later in life. Maybe Pete misunderstood the story or it lost something in cocktail party translation—just another snippet for the voluminous Hogan file. Perhaps this disclosure will trigger other reminiscences.

The statuesque pose of Hogan finishing his swing at Merion in 1950 is a monument to grace under fire. Little wonder the poster remains so popular, as timeless in its way as *Five Lessons*. A more personal, indelible memory of Hogan comes not from the lens of either Hy Peskin and Jules Alexander but from a brief encounter of the icon on a much less majestic stage.

Hogan was seated behind a table at the annual trade show hosted by the PGA of America in the early nineties. Public appearances for Hogan were far from an everyday occurrence. The show is closed to the public but PGA members, eager for a brush with greatness, deferentially took their place in the long line that formed.

A quirky memory surfaced as I paused to watch. Dissolve to Macy's in Manhattan some years earlier. Budweiser eighties icon Spuds MacKenzie, the phlegmatic British bull terrier, was in store "signing" autographs. The line of admirers stretched through several departments causing a store employee to shake his head in amazement. "This is longer than [for] Gloria Vanderbilt," he said. One notices these things and the only line I ever witnessed from years of attending the cavernous trade show that came anywhere close to equaling the wait for Hogan was, if a distant second, for LPGA great Patty Berg. Even from a distance, Hogan's ease and good nature were apparent, counter-balanced by the genuine excitement of those waiting anxiously to briefly pay their respects and secure an autograph. Such was Hogan's celebrity that people who couldn't get in the line still stopped just to watch him sign.

There are always more pressing things to do at the PGA Show than watch an elderly man sign autographs, even for a freelance writing bottom-feeder, but that changed after spying an individual about eight back in the queue. He wasn't a biker; this was, after all, a PGA Show where the crowd is laughably homogeneous—golf pros plucked as if straight from Central Casting—looks, shined shoes, hair, clothes, gait by FootJoy —but this guy was different. He sported a ponytail! And he was wearing faded jeans, certainly not the typical uniform of a PGA member looking sharp, and not exactly radiating the Hogan dress code.

A quick aside. The consumer Darrell Survey confirms that year after year t-shirts remain the number one shirt in golf, out-distancing Cutter & Buck, Ashworth and the other trendsetters. The professional golfer remains sport's most fastidious and well-dressed athlete (the stereotypical predilection for flagrant patterns notwithstanding). The impending decline of the collar may be genuine cause for concern in some quarters but golf fashion is ever evolving. Times change. An editorial writer in the British *Golf Illustrated* of May 17, 1901, chuffed: "I devoutly hope that the American custom of playing golf in *shirtsleeves* will never obtain in this country. If the weather is too hot for a flannel jacket, it is too hot for golf." The poor chap was thankfully spared later degradations.)

The line towards Hogan slowly advanced. How would the great man who exhibited such care that he eschewed zippers on his trousers for buttons, and added extra cleat holes on his golf shoes (16 each!), deal with a slacker in jeans and a pony tail? The stories of his icy disposition are reknown; he did not suffer fools gladly. I'll tell you what he did. Ben Hogan looked the man in the eye, smiled, thanked him, shook his hand, and signed a poster. For want of a definition of a consummate professional, I would suggest that most days that will do.

two

•••••mastering the fundamentals••••

pickin' it up pro-style!

No pro worth the callus at the base of his pinky would risk a shot in competition that he hadn't practiced. Yet there you amateurs go *winging* your way through a move that imperils the lower back, glutes, knees, and wrists. Master this fundamental to build confidence. It also favorably impacts slow play and avoids embarrassing *plumber's crack*.

There's no reason why you can't share the assuredness of the pros in removing the ball from the hole. What's their secret? How do they move with élan of ballet dancers, adept at the Full Egret and the Limbo Low Knee Flex?

For starters, they rarely lift anything heavier than a fork, a shoe bag or the occasional weighted club. They also apply the three (make that four) Ps, one R and a GF to success: Practice, Good Footwork, Plan, Pirouette and Review (and, occasionally, Prevaricate).

Study the following sequence. Practice the moves in front of a mirror to restful music (and, ideally, short bursts of deferential applause). Mimic Tiger through his paces. Trust. You might also practice that other P: which stands for Push-Away, as in desserts. And, for god's sakes, go

easy on the ACL! Your author does not want any lawsuits or candidates for arthroscopic surgery. He knows you're too cheap to take a lesson, but with our exclusive tips you too can pick it up pro style!

We join the young Tiger having already assumed several optimal positions: his shoulders are square to the target line, his arms are comfortably extended from the body, his eyes are intently focused on the hole as the left foot simultaneously prepares to plant—the result of a satisfactory and commendable weight shift. His trousers could stand pressing, one hesitates to add, but this was in Tiger's "burger and shakes" period. Clearly, practicing this critical move for years under his father's tutelage has paid off. For the uninitiated, two words: mirror work.

Tiger's casual extension from the waist produces a slight "hump back," a not extraordinary position for a man of his height, if not exactly neo-classical form. Not too much should be made as this interim set is over in an instant. The putter is solidly planted (where so many errors are made) with a relaxed if slightly unorthodox right forefinger set. This instinctual move should not be copied by the less skilled. Let it happen. If it does, fine. If not, it just looks forced.

Particular attention should be paid to what some might consider evidence of a "lazy" left knee. Here it appears to be trailing slightly. This in turn necessitates that the knee buttress the full weight of the body, and comes at a cost even with a spectacular athlete like Tiger. His left arm continues very much "on plane," what the experts recognize as a superb anticipatory angle of inclination (patent pending). Tiger's right foot has also levitated—just so—again, perfectly acceptable with this caveat—*if it wants to*—without affectation.

The classic forward retrieval posture common to all the greats, Tiger here is clearly "staying within himself." You can feel that, can't you? For those less accomplished: Start with three sets of five reps before the round then work up progressively to 10 or so, careful not to overdo it or to gloss over the fundamental checkpoints previously highlighted. (Important: Always check with your personal physician before beginning this or any exercise regimen.)

Ripples at the base of the shirt attest to the stress placed on the lower back but the dominant player of his era displays the individual style honed from years of dedicated application. How do you get to Carnegie Hall or Augusta National? Practice, practice, practice!

Tiger strikes a statuesque "Full Egret" posture positively brimming with confidence. Critics have questioned—unfairly, I believe—his "flying" right elbow in this stage of the retrieval process. They are clueless, jealous perhaps of his technique, or their own limited ability. His terrific past parallel extension exemplifies his exceptional flexibility. Again, this doesn't happen without dedication worthy of a champion. Bravo! Take a bow.

The moment of truth where even the best preparation can go for naught if the hands get too 'grabby.' Tiger uncharacteristically "ice cream cones" his ball here but he gets away with it owing to his superb athleticism. Few among us would be so fortunate. The frame reveals an unsettling momentary uncertainty. Will he drop the ball? Will he lose his concentration and topple over or scuff the green? His conditioning and finesse keep him in balance. A lesser-skilled practitioner frequently loses 'it' here.

Much…much better. Back in synch, back in control, res-cued by supreme internal timing. You can't expect results like this overnight, even with this expert and expensive instruction. Tiger's right foot prepares to swing into posi-tion, just as it should, the ball is secure in the fingers but not too tight (loose fist). The left knee again bears the weight before straightening.

Our work here is done. Mission accomplished, thanks in part to today's breathable fabrics. The high-speed photography verifies modern casual fashion's disdain for the pre-dip trouser tuck. Past generations of golfers were all too familiar with this hardship having to adapt, sometimes awkwardly, to a fixture of previous eras now fairly gone the way of the stymie and the stiff collar.

when golf is no fun

With few exceptions, the touring pro's devotion to order clearly separates Us from Them. Ben Hogan, for instance, was exceedingly punctual and always well dressed. His professional look, muted colors, with trousers tailored to remove troublesome zippers for buttons evidence of his meticulous preparation. The story of his arriving on the steps at Seminole Country Club at the same time each morning is an established (and accurate) part of the man's mystique. Apparently you could set your watch to it. It's not an original thought but Hogan's ability to compartmentalize the various aspects of his life: his family, tragic past, golf, business and social life must surely be regarded as an enormous asset. For his successors, more or less, the same is true.

Harvey Penick believed that Hogan played so well because he knew *his* swing better than everyone else knew *theirs*. Biographer Curt Sampson concurs by suggesting that the real Hogan secret lay in the depth of his own understanding. Undoubtedly, this is wise counsel in any endeavor, a variation on *Polonius's* advice "to thine own self be true." Now, as to whether William Shakespeare appreciated or even contemplated the difficulties of, say, a downhill, sidehill three-foot putt, records are incomplete. His association with golf remains another mystery of his personal life. We do know the Bard penned "Good words are better than bad strokes" (*Julius Caesar*, v.I.). Another favorite from an amusing list compiled in *Golfiana*: "O, cursed be the hand that made these holes!" from *Richard III* (i. 2.).

Such obsession to routine broaches a difficult question. Is regimentation imperative to golfing excellence? A chilling prospect for those partial to t-shirts and routinely late for tee times, ample evidence suggests an orderly penchant may be nothing less than a fundamental. Distracted once over the ball, hall of famer Billy Casper would completely rewind, fully starting over the preamble that would lead to his striking the ball by returning his golf club back to its slot in the bag. One current

PGA Tour player hits exactly the same number of practice balls before his round, the same number allotted to the same clubs every time. Never varies. The volatile former LPGA star Dottie Pepper had a formidable pre-shot routine. A natural extension of her fiery personality in microcosm, it was as individual as a thumbprint. She seemed to stalk her ball before hitting it. One foot placed slightly in front of the other, her club pointed in the air like a rifle sight, she stood tall emitting the bravado of a toreador. Of course, such precise deliberations can make the pros appallingly slow in contravention to the spirit and letter of the rules. They will actually practice their pre-shot routine to the second, to the point of developing several settings in the event of their being so slow that they are placed "on the clock."

This was not always the case. Champion golfers once played without so much as a waggle. Early British champion George Duncan barely slowed down to hit the ball. His autobiography was aptly titled: "Golf at the Gallop." 'Miss 'em Quick' was the old adage. Would scores today improve with faster play? I believe they would.

The madness is that we're taught that deliberation instills comfort and strength. For most of us, it must be said, a sense of order is as elusive on—as off—the golf course. Whether the inability to bend time to their will is to blame for the radiating moodiness and severity of most touring pros is for the psychologists to answer. How rare it is that anyone's schedule goes precisely as planned. No wonder they're crabby. Annika Sorenstam once found herself stuck in traffic on the way to a U.S. Open round, and then had a flat tire. That would likely be enough to unravel most mortals. She had the superior mental strength to set it all aside, go out and win, a truly impressive, Hogan-esque display of compartmentalizing.

Then there is J.D. After disabling his recreational vehicle in a MacDonald's drive-thru by getting it stuck on the gate (it exceeded height restrictions), John Daly, in danger of missing his tee time, called the tournament office requesting back-up. A police escort was dispatched. To avoid the tournament traffic, the convoy navigated a highway access road from the wrong direction. John did not win that week but he made his tee time. His bumbling and genial manner (giving every appearance of a high state of disorganization—yay!) may go far in explaining his popularity despite an accumulating list of transgressions. Or, it may just be that the rules are different for anyone who can hit a sand wedge 115 yards. There is a more serious side to Daly's Ruthian excesses but he has his majors, his fans, and an appealing country personality of a Southern boy who learned early in life that forgiveness is always easier to receive than permission. As in all sports, in golf stubbornness is often fortifying and enriching. That the pros grind away applying heaping amounts of convention and order to solve an unconventional and anarchic riddle may partly explain why golf can't be conquered. The round peg of discipline doesn't always fit inside the square hole of a game where luck, despite Man's best efforts, refuses to be go away.

The pro golfer's ability to forget—if not to forgive—at least to set aside the inevitable slings and arrows—also distinguishes their success. (Harvey Penick believed that a little deafness in a golfer was also not such a bad thing.) What happened yesterday or last year, the previous shot, a flat tire, the slights and demons real or imagined, at their best they can work through it. Ouimet never heard the horns blaring from the traffic jam directly behind him as he sank the snaking putt to win the U.S. Open. In similar circumstances, Joyce Wethered never heard the locomotive's approach.

"What train?" she asked.

The flip side to such positive focus can be just as consuming. Bob Jones described the intense pressure as feeling as if "running from something without knowing what or where it is," a harrowing state. Still, examples abound of those who have triumphed by reaching beyond the fear into a transcendent state of clarity. "My mind became perfectly clear, my memory was sharp and precise..." Arnold Palmer confided after the 1966 British Open. "I felt tremendously charged up and yet absolutely calm and self-possessed at the same time. It was a very strange experience."

Monetary concerns are always near the surface, particularly for those trapped into validating their existence by the harsh barometer of their standing on the official money list. But it's not—solely, anyway—about the money. It's their stubborn, eccentric personal quest, disparate and at times alienating, that those of us who watch and play golf recreationally just don't quite *get*.

"I know there are people who regard me as off-hand and even surly when I am playing golf," wrote Bobby Locke. "But, golf is my business."

It is a cornerstone of golf that the very good amateur seldom beats the professional. Jim Thorpe, a self-described hustler who has enjoyed considerable success on the Champion's Tour, has a ready explanation.

> Most of us have learned to accept the miss and leave it there and go on and execute the next shot. I think the amateur guy kind of takes that shot with him. "Oh, if I hadn't three-putted that green, I would be this...If I hadn't chili-dipped that shot..." We don't think about it because we have played so much, we have learned to accept it.

The past presents one burden, the future another. Expectations are a cruel, tantalizing carrot. A clinical psychologist who works with golfers shares the story of a touring pro client (they don't call them patients). He was so bedeviled by the thought of missing short putts that, before he even drew back the blade, he heard the groan of the crowd for the putt that *just* slides by the hole—that awful half-sigh, half-groan.

Few amateur golfers could feel anything but sympathy for Thomas "Boo" Weekly. Hard to root against anyone named Boo, his past, present and future merged in a moment of public poignancy. At the 2007 Honda Classic, he had the proverbial putt to win but could not coax a 39" putt into the hole.

"The nerves got me," he confided. "This is all a dream. I was shakin'. I ain't going to lie to you. I mean, I was shakin' like a leaf. My hands were, like, numb." Boo's boo-boo offered a monumental fork in the road, from which some recover while others are never heard from again.

"Perhaps it is because golf is really such a lonely, selfish game," Gary Player wrote in 1962, "that it breeds so many lonely, selfish people."

Loneliness is not exclusive to golf, of course. Aside from the weight of expectations and the excruciating pain after the simplest putt is missed, perhaps only one similar torment comes close. Would that it could provide some comfort, even to the golfer who anticipates the groan of missed putts. Jacques Plante, the hall of fame Canadiens goalie, once described letting in a cheap goal this way.

> Imagine yourself sitting in an office and you make an error of some kind—call it an error of judgment or a mistake over the phone. All of a sudden, behind you, a bright light goes on, the walls collapse and there are eighteen thousand people shouting and jeering at you, calling you an imbecile and an idiot and a bum and throwing things at you, including garbage.

Muhammad Ali imagined the private humiliation of a knock-out leading him to a room inhabited by alligators wearing top hats and playing trombones. It is a fanciful image that would not be amiss in a Hieronymous Bosch depiction of the delights of Hell.

To their credit the lonely and selfish manage to suppress their darker urges, thus avoiding the daily criminal blotter of big-time sports. Knock on wood, pro golf is still a kitten by comparison, a stream that remains clear, cool and running. No rock star green M&M tantrums,

TV sets flying through windows, rarely anything worse than a snubbed handshake, a curt interview, and a killing glare. On an awful assignment late in the season, I once had to ambulance-chase players for comments about Tiger's upcoming year. Short of being asked about cheating on their wives, there are few things PGA Tour players relish more then being asked about someone else. Charles Howell III gave me the appropriate and expected response. Still his intensity stopped me in my tracks. How would Tiger do? "Ask Tiger," he said, barely breaking stride. Another player told me, again appropriately, "How the #$@%! should I know?"

Occasionally Tiger's more colorful expressions are inadvertently shared; he rues the long-distance mics that capture and transmit his every word. During the final round of his second Open win at St. Andrews, the observant viewer heard him mouth a most interesting phrase. Why, it was none other than John McEnroe's infamous rant over an objectionable call at Wimbledon, the memorable (and later determined steroid-induced): "You CAN'T be serious!" Tiger, however, said it almost under his breath. The pervading sense of decorum and intense concentration, so easily overlooked in the nano-second blitz of sports highlights, underpins golf at its unplugged best. What other professional sport begins and ends with a genuine handshake between competitors?

Pro golfers genuinely mistrust the media but that hardly qualifies as unusual. The media, fans and pro-am partners—over-enthusiastic, imbecilic, well-meaning if unruly—are lamentable occupational hazards. The fans are closer, always within earshot and more capable of intruding into the golfer's sense of order than in any other big-time sport. For the real golf fan to unavoidably cast a shadow across the 71st tee box at the Masters as the leader tees off is enough to quicken the pulse. Fans have allegiances but they also cheer for the game and a fair, deserving winner. What of an inopportune sneeze on the backswing, a mosquito sting, a sudden movement? Mindfulness is then at a premium; no real golf fan wants to be anything more than a witness to the Boo Weeklies of the world confronting their destiny.

The most knowledgeable fans must be in the crowd for an Open Championship at St. Andrews. In 2000, two elderly gentlemen, dressed in suits and overcoats, sat together in the stands overlooking the Road Hole green, with its spectacular view out across the course. Not a word passed between them. Most players prudently play the dangerous hole by laying up to avoid the bunker. They then chip on or finesse a short pitch to leave them with a reasonable effort at saving par with one putt. These safe if unexciting tactics elicited no comment from the two elderly spectators as group after group played through. Ernie Els then appeared back in the fairway. He made a very bold play and his beautiful mid-iron approach painted the flag stopping six feet from the hole, cut just over the maw of the bunker. It was a spectacular shot!

"Good shot," one gent said quietly, without turning.

"Aye," said the other.

That was their only exchange in two hours. God love 'em. They would be lost in the 700 level or among the painted faces in the 'dog pound,' doing the *wave* or banging plastic sticks together behind the basket to distract someone from sinking a free throw.

Golf's next pervasive scandal will be its first, and undoubtedly white collar in nature. The tour's tight reins, tradition, and the self-enforced premium placed on individual responsibility and honor have spared us. Conspiracies can only happen among conspirators not among competitors. Mistakes can be made but cheating remains a deliberate act, and few survive conviction.

The emphasis on personal conduct and control—extended to such things as ball flight, emotions, distance, schedule—can take on Puritanical expression. The tour's aversion to seeing players' and caddies' knees and ankles, for instance, seems a dangerous extravagance in hot, humid weather. Would not the game and the players be better served by letting those who want to wear shorts do so, and instead enforcing the long-standing rules on pace of play?

The best golfers in the world are certainly skilled in keeping their emotions in check. Their restraint calls to mind a pattern of human behavior addressed by that master psychologist, the late comedian Rodney Dangerfield. He had a telling routine centered on an individual he called the "quiet man." The quiet man is a staple of criminal activity. After so many unspeakable crimes are uncovered, the scoundrel unmasked and hauled away, the neighbors are certain to be interviewed, he observed. Unfailingly, the criminal is described as an unobtrusive neighbor who went about his business and kept to himself. He was "a quiet man." Not that the PGA Tour harbors closet psychotics but most are decidedly quiet men. The impression given is that they're devoutly studious, "tightly wound," or as one player diplomatically described a veteran colleague, "high-maintenance." Many years ago Ben Wright, the excommunicated television voice, wrote a wonderful story about a golfer who literally snaps with only a tiddler left to win the championship. *Twilight Hour*, a fictional autobiographical account, ends with the player confined to an institution.

Several prominent golfers have tragically struggled with mental disorders more serious than the yips or other golf afflictions. Twice a U.S. Open champion, and the winner remarkably as a teenager, Johnny McDermott landed in the sanitarium. A tragic tale, his downward spiral apparently began with a stunning, impolitic burst of bravado. He was merely ahead of his time. Today, no one would bat an eyelid at such behavior.

"All I can say," boasted a cocky Paula Creamer, 19, before her Solheim Cup debut, "is that they [the European team] better get ready, because they're going to get beat." Later, given a chance to modify her remarks, she said only: "I may have gotten ahead of myself but I am ready to win. I said what I needed to say."

McDermott was crucified for saying as much. Of course there remains an indistinct line between confidence and cockiness. In his day, he clearly crossed it. Even before he burst on the national scene, A.W. Tillinghast noted Johnny's "supreme egotism." J.J. could play, there was no doubt. "He feared no man," wrote Tillinghast, "and his self-assurance was supreme." The week before the 1913 U.S. Open, in the Poconos of Pennsylvania, McDermott bested all the top players, Harry Vardon and Ted Ray among them. Receiving his medal, McDermott responded to calls for a speech from the crowd. The "Little American Boy" told those assembled, including the illustrious opponents standing before him, "that none need fear that the Open title would go across the seas," that more of the same medicine would be dispensed at Brookline. That was the extent of it. Tillinghast, course architect, early American golf advocate and friend of the British stars, listened and was mortified. Reporters were asked to hold off on the story but it was too hot. The USGA threatened McDermott for his incendiary remarks with censure. Subsequent editorials raked him over the coals. There is a pathetic photo taken shortly after the incident. McDermott stares downward flanked by the two great British golfers of his age. According to Tillinghast, the incident "broke" the young man's spirit. "He turned up at Brookline, but played like a dead man. His indifferent performance was so far below his normal game that it showed how terribly his mind was upset. There was absolutely no life, no sting to his shots-then, or ever again." Tillie said the subsequent publicity was "the rat which gnawed the foundation timbers of one of the greatest golf games ever produced in America." Could the bullying remarks have obscured a fragile insecurity? *The Times* merely referred to Creamer's "remarkable confidence" and warned she might very well back up her boasts, as she proved convincingly. McDermott's collapse obviously took place long ago in a far different cultural context.

It is curious that several small courses adjoin state mental facilities in various parts of the country. A fine example can be found in the small

town of Chattahoochee, Florida. Just past the prison and the horticul-
tural therapy buildings is a lovely nine-hole course surrounded by tall
pines bedecked with Spanish moss. Two golfing gentlemen showed me
around. One of had a pronounced Scottish brogue which I assumed
was genuine. Whether they were town residents, or had some more
formal relationship with the larger facilities for which Chattahoochee
is known, I was not going to ask. They were congenial company, and
I will never forget driving through the rural Florida panhandle stopping to ask directions. It was a lonely gas station, the office of which
was positively brimming with men and boys who looked like they'd
been there all day, and might very well have all been related.
Conversation ceased upon my arrival. Eyes narrowed when I asked for
directions to the home of the state mental hospital. Whether golf can
provide some relief and comfort to those struggling with their sanity
is a question I don't feel equipped to answer. Its diverting qualities are
well known. Perhaps those institutionalized can find solace in appreciating Irish essayist Robert Lynd's observation that "It is almost
impossible to remember how tragic a place the world is when one is
playing golf."

The course, incidentally, is still there, although the state legislature
several years ago was asking questions about its finances. If you're passing that way, nine-holes are recommended as is leaving time for the
amusing detour of scaring the locals by asking directions.

Perhaps a heightened sense of order may keep the golfer's personal
demons in check for as long as humanly possible. We do know that
eccentrics generally lead happy lives. Would it come as a surprise to find
golfers so meticulous in their approach to golf and to life that they—as
one eccentric British lawyer was alleged to have done—measure breakfast
strips of bacon sending back those deemed non-conforming? In the precise world of the touring pro, conformity is as safe and nurturing as a
sound pre-shot routine. "He's never on time for anything but golf,"

Barbara Nicklaus once said of her husband. Somehow that's comforting to know.

Travel's grind on those who play the game for a living is sorely underestimated, at least by those looking in from outside. Unpleasantries threaten even the best laid plans. Maybe the preoccupation with having everything just so is the inevitable reaction to the tour player's daily struggles. Golf toys with Type A personalities sending them chasing after perfection's tail. But they can no more control the game's uncertainties than they can assure the fate of their luggage. A New Zealand touring pro once arrived in Europe after traveling halfway around the world. (He was without a shared or privately-owned jet, another advance in insulating themselves from the intrusions of daily life, though, as we know, not without its own problems). Rushing to play his round, he returned to a hotel in a foreign country where he did not speak the language, to a room without sheets or towels. Exhausted and hungry, weary from jet-lag, he merely took a shower and collapsed.

These trials may help explain why their diffidence and occasional malevolence serves as a shield. The ideal is exemplified by comments Henry Longhurst once made regarding five-time Open champion Peter Thomson (1958), often repeated in ensuing years in lauding the better player. "...And the highest compliment one can pay him," Longhurst wrote, "is to say that the newly-arrived spectator could not tell from his mien or demeanor whether he had just lost a stroke or gained one." Boring, perhaps, but ultimately less stressful to the system.

Theirs is a volatile and predatory world. Those who scoff at golf as a sport need to remember there is no safety net, no team hug, no guarantees, not even a bubbling inflated mascot. The stories of struggling touring pros sleeping in cars, or even bunkers, foraging among the mini tours, *this close* to going back to selling car stereos or golf balls or insurance hit very close to home. There is always a shot at redemption for the batter who strikes out, the pitcher who gets shelled, the safety burned for a touchdown. Someone may pick him up. The team may still win the game. He's still under contract. He still gets paid. His miseries are communal.

No so for the pro golfer for whom home games are rare. There are unfailing courtesies and luxuries, for sure, from tickets to anything in town, to a concierge looking after the wife and kids, and occasional free travel (and, a personal favorite perk taken for granted, new balls of their preference waiting on the range), but theirs is a solitary quest, and no one can begrudge them their keep.

Tom Kite, who I've observed flying steerage, for a time maintained an occasional if, for some, disquieting presence on the PGA Tour. He had a telling reminder for those questioning his motives. "I haven't been playing for the fans or the skeptics," he said in explaining his breaks from the Champions Tour, clearly not content to play quietly with the other seniors. Why is that so hard to understand, he seemed to say. Why don't YOU get it? "I've been playing for myself. I'm playing because I love to play the game. I don't really care what the so-called experts say, one way or the other." That constant has burned brightly deep inside from his days of thick glasses and disc-creaking reverse C swing. He could've been a 49'er headed into the mountains beside a loaded burro. And this from one of the game's all-time leading money winners who's already successfully worked his claim, once for years the leading earner on tour.

Tiger Woods's work ethic is largely obscured by his efforts at maintaining privacy. Bryan Gathright who coaches Notah Begay III, a former teammate of Tiger's at Stanford, tells of trying to beat the world's No. 1 player to the golf course. Bryan and Notah arrived at dawn for a practice round with Tiger, who likes to get his business done early and be gone, beating the crowds. It was hardly light enough to see a ball land, but when they arrived Tiger had already teed off. "He just doesn't wait," said Bryan. This happened more than once so the two hashed a plan one year at the Memorial.

"We got there long before daylight and were waiting. We had some breakfast and were thinking we had him," Bryan said. "It turned out Tiger had already been there and been out warming up on the putting green. He'd just come in and grabbed a bowl of cereal or a banana, or something, and just gone to the putting green. I told Notah, 'Maybe we ought to just spend the night there and see if he's actually sleeping at the golf course because I'm not sure that wasn't the case!'"

Not once during 1999 or 2000 could they beat Tiger to the office. "It didn't seem to matter what time we said we were going to be there. He was there fifteen or twenty minutes earlier."

The topper came after Tiger's remarkable come-back win for the PGA Championship at Valhalla, the third piece of the so-called Tiger Slam. Notah had not had a chance to congratulate his friend so he called Tiger on Monday morning at 9:20 Eastern. Notah could hear wind whistling through the cell phone and he asked Tiger where he was. Tiger was out on the range at Isleworth in Orlando hitting balls. Considering that his obligations as PGA Champion in Louisville, Kentucky the day before included the inevitable media interviews, a reception and flight home, he probably got in around 2 a.m., perhaps in bed by three. Here he was the next morning punching the clock after a stunning, no doubt exhausting victory in a major?! Are you kidding me?! The great New Orleans musician Allen Toussaint once mentioned that he starts his day at the Steinway. "That's how I say good morning to myself," he said. It must be the same with the maestros of golf so dedicated that they can't wait to say good morning to themselves by practicing their scales even the morning after an exhausting gig.

Long forgotten, a generational tiff briefly existed between Kite and Woods about how much golf a 21-year old on tour could play. Tom thought a lot more, as he once set the standard for a workaholic. Tiger had his own ideas, though the two must share much more in common regarding their work ethic than they have in disagreement. The old pro made a subtle dig about Tiger's limited playing schedule. One of Tiger's first professional events was in San Antonio in 1996, a marvelous, festive occasion that transcended golf. Tickets couldn't be printed fast enough. Several fans admitted they'd never before been to a pro golf event, giddy with themselves for even being there. One had obviously come directly from work. Lining the 18th fairway for a glimpse, he stood dressed in his white chef's jacket and toque.

After his round as he waited for the formal press conference to begin, I shouted through the din asking Tiger about his plans for the upcoming holidays. In the crunch of a jammed and inadequate media tent, the meaning changed. By the time he fielded it, the question had become: "What are your plans for the off-season?" He looked blankly ahead, with what I imagine was the same you-just-don't-get-it look that Kite expressed with his tightly pursed lips when he made his statement about continuing to play on the PGA Tour past his prime. "Golf doesn't have an off-season," deadpanned Tiger. It may never again.Δ58

As the years roll on it appears the Ryder Cup plagues him as an intriguing Achilles' heel. Match play is notoriously unpredictable, one reason why the event is so compelling, and I would suggest one reason why golf initially thrived. Luck may be the residue of design, but less so in match than in medal play. The pros prefer the more stable continuity from 72 holes of stroke play. In match play, upsets are the norm, as Tiger well knows. Jack Nicklaus was repeatedly taken to the wire by one Maurice Bembridge and lost, famously, twice in the same day to journeyman Brian Barnes. "The greatest player in history" at one point had a less than golden 1-5 record in singles matches; it was the Barnes defeat that prompted a Fleet Street wag to marvel: "What was Nicklaus trying to do, anyway, get Barnes a Knighthood? Or a tickertape parade down Piccadilly?" It should be obligatory when mentioning that defeat to highlight Nicklaus's response, another reason that Jack merits his exalted reputation. After losing in the afternoon 2 and 1, he congratulated

Barnes then went to the U.S. side of the locker room. "That was it," Barnes later recalled. "He took defeat as you would expect the greatest golfer in the world would. He took it like a gentleman."

Tiger's total package: his determination to catch the Nicklaus record, his catty retorts that no one remembers Jack's Ryder Cup record (17-8-3), his careful upbringing, all point in the same unerring direction—away from the concept of team. That's golf. A Tiger can't change his stripes. It may be too incongruous, uncomfortable and unwelcome a distraction to pair him for a week every couple of years (or annually with the Presidents Cup) with those he seeks to dominate and expect everything to go swimmingly. The Ryder Cup is just not a priority for him and his lackluster results reflect it.

One PGA Tour stalwart, a Texan no less, well aware of Hogan's shadow, memorably exercises control over, of all things, his closets. We were awaiting his arrival when his wife provided us with the thrilling details. A prodigious clotheshorse, he was also a regular Felix Unger carefully arranging trousers and shirts by color in his closet and drawers—robin egg blues with robin egg blues and so on. His fetish amused the media types who nobly uphold their reputation as slobs. Golf writers long ago jettisoned ties or even blazers. They wouldn't recognize an iron that didn't have a number etched on the bottom. The worst offenders arrive in cutoffs and t-shirt, in contrast to those they cover residents of a world where everything, down to their closet, is just so. It is an orderly universe if an imperfect world, where at least one pro washes the rental car before returning it, an action that I'm certain has never occurred to any golf writer.

For the vast majority of recreational golfers, neither their closets or their golf conveys even the illusion of order. We can only hope that good play does not require such exactitude. That John Daly refused to don a blazer "on a fat man" to attend a champions dinner at St. Andrews likely heartened those who find Sansabelt less amusing a concept than they'd care to admit.

Wise counsel on the subject of golf apparel comes from two unlikely sources. Those of a certain age will remember Dino Danelli, the drummer and leader of the Young Rascals, a sixties band back when stemming the British Invasion was serious business. The Rascals consented to wear a ridiculous uniform inflicted upon them by their manager—hokey school boy outfits complete with winged collars, striped knickers and wacky, wide, old-fashioned ties. For a guy from Jersey City into the blues it was …humiliating. "We got on stage and got laughed at *until we started playing,*" Danelli told fellow drummer Max Weinberg. Therein lies a moral. Those with game are afforded considerable license. Not that it always works for the pros. As my old muny pro Joe Balander told me many times: "You can't teach style." May there always be courses where the dress code can be easily communicated. At the somewhat downmarket Cedars of Bergstrom in Austin, the policy was expressed by Jack Marr, a third generation pro and younger brother of the classy PGA Champion and commentator. "Whatever it is," advised Jack, "keep it on. Just keep it on."

Perhaps it's being in Texas that makes Ben Hogan still seem so relevant and impermeable a presence. His table in the corner of the Shady Oaks dining room, and his locker still await his return. Next to the pro shop at Colonial, his office has been painstakingly recreated. There's a vicarious thrill lingering there, studying the photos, opening the drawers. Hogan seems to have just stepped away. A hacked up competitor's golf ball, opened to survey its innards, stills rolls around when the bottom left-hand drawer is examined. The office is a little unsettling. It's as if he might appear at any moment.

Naturally, I had to poke around. The contents of Ben Hogan's middle right desk drawer:

> Rolaids, Isoptofrin (eye drops), Tiger Balm (Singapore), Glazcote (for lenses), Sucrets, Vicks Cough Silencers, Dristan, Tylenol, Lotion Soft body cream, Lotion Soft skin conditioner, Nupercainal ointment.

Hogan stories span the touching to the heinous. It is curious with larger than life figures that, as with Ben Hogan, the expanding library devoted to his life has done little to quell curiosity. The conversation has been steered and stemmed, yet like a river that refuses Man's best intentions, the Hogan myth follows its own course. Given the intensity of the scrutiny, isn't it interesting that a haze still obscures the man?

His invention of practice is one aspect of his myth, maybe the only one; or, there may be others—that is unfair. His dedication was legendary. Would it be enough to say that he simply enjoyed the pleasure of being alone with his thoughts, a stick and ball? There is another simple explanation for his drive, true enough of other disciplines, succinctly expressed by the opera singer Birgit Nilsson: "To be satisfied with oneself is the greatest danger in an artist's life." Hogan, I don't believe, was ever willing to permit himself that satisfaction. Nor, for that matter, is Tiger.

His dedication was no artifice, but it does nothing to diminish the Hogan mystique to put it in context. Golfers throughout history have spared no effort. Al Watrous, an early professional, Ryder Cup star and Canadian Open champion, was said to hit 500 balls a day, this in the Jones era. Watrous went on to become the head pro at Oakland Hills in Detroit, and is the subject of an interesting footnote with respect to conceding putts in match play. He lost the 1932 PGA Championship after being nine holes up with eleven to play. He remembered that it all began unraveling after he innocently conceded his opponent Bobby Cruickshank a six-footer. (Memo to Self: Never concede a six-footer.)

Across the Atlantic, at about the same time Watrous was winning or nearly winning tournaments—while Hogan was still in the caddie yard —Archie Compston was hard at it, described as a "...a grim, determined player, deadly serious, and often in the morning he goes out with a bucketful of balls and works at his shots for hours." Three-time British Open champion Henry Cotton was said to practice for nine hours at a stretch. Canadian swing savant Moe Norman would later hit 600 balls a day over the course of twenty years. Pipeline Moe would fill his bag with balls and carry it around, even during tournaments, to build up strength in his legs. For all we know, Young Tom Morris did his due diligence. Tom Kite, to name another ascetic, certainly has. Even Walter Hagen, whose name was initially confused with Hogan in the papers, as the young Texan made a name for himself, was no slouch. Renowned for his partying image, Hagen was, in fact, an expert "drink hider." If it didn't make as appealing a story as the Haig turning up on the first tee in a crumpled tuxedo (crumpled as part of a ruse), he, as have succeeding generations of pros, looked upon the course as their office. Golf was indeed their job. Hagen was justifiably proud about his dedication, writing in his autobiography:

> *I worked as hard to perfect my golf game as any other fellow would work in his brokerage office, in his job as a mechanic in a garage, as a lawyer or as a traveling salesman. My game was my business and as a business it demanded consistent playing in the championship bracket, for a current title was my selling commodity.*

One of the few golfers who succeeded Hogan that he openly respected was fellow Texan Lee Trevino, and it is difficult to imagine anyone working harder.

Here Trevino describes his routine early on:

> *I was 25 years old, married, with a child, and all I'm thinking about is putting food on the table and paying the rent, drinking beer every night and raising hell with all of my friends there at the club. If it was day-light at 5:30 or 4:30, I'd get up and go out to chip and putt at 4:30 in the morning. Or, if it was dark, I'd hit the balls towards the west because that's the lightest area and I could still see the ball. (laughs) Don't hit them east because you can't see them. I'd hit them west, where the sun was setting and that sky is nice*

*and gold, and you can still see the ball. I did this seven days
a week. I mean, I never missed. I've gotten up in the morning with some of the damnest hangovers, too. I'd go to bed
sometimes at three in the morning but I'd still get up at five
to hit balls. But I did it not because I was thinking of the
U.S. Open, or of this or that. All I wanted to do was beat
that guy the next day.*

At the risk of sounding churlish, with respect to Tiger's place in history,
until he gets his ride through the Canyon of Heroes in Lower
Manhattan, a tribute accorded both Hogan and Jones, perhaps it's best if
we hold off for now. He still has a long way to go to catch Jack's record
of major championships. Two other records it's doubtful he'll ever match:
Jack Nicklaus's participation in a record 44 U.S. Opens, and the six-
decade relationship Gene Sarazen had with Wilson Sporting Goods. Just
a thought.

ViJay Singh has come to set a certain modern standard. This too is
no act. Before dawn at a Tour Championship, while the marshals were
still arriving, drinking coffee and downing doughnuts, ViJay was on the
practice green. Mind you, it was still nearly pitch dark; his tee time was-
n't until mid-morning. He waited patiently practice putting without a
ball on the fringe, thick with early morning dew. When it got light
enough to putt two-footers, he did so. When it was light enough to putt
longer putts, he moved back to stroke five and six-foot putts, only paus-
ing to allow a mower to make its passes. As the day beckoned and the
light improved he moved in gradations to hitting longer shots, short
chips, then short pitches. The quiet was still pervasive, the tournament
just awakening. When it got light enough to follow a ball in flight, albeit
a wedge or short iron, he walked slowly over to the deserted, fog shroud-
ed practice area, joined now by his caddie, solitary figures punching the
clock on the uninhabited range. His only current rival, not un-coinciden-
tally, has been Tiger. I suspect Vijay, like Hogan and those consumed by

their research, enjoys being left alone with his thoughts, sticks and balls, and uses his swing as a way of saying good morning to himself.

It's always interesting when instructional wisdom appears to conflict. Here are two apparent contradictions over the value of practice:

> *What I've learned is that when a fellow is hitting the golf ball well he should try to keep in that groove until it becomes a habit. —Ben Hogan*

> *Nothing can be gained by tinkering with your swing after it has been once straightened out. —Bob Jones*

Of course, they're both right. Each statement speaks to the different personalities of each man as much as to their different approaches to playing golf.

Hogan's reflections need to be sipped and savored rather than gulped. His contemporary, Byron Nelson was as admirable an individual as golf has ever nurtured. His records are fantastic, his legacy as genuine as his tournament's commitment to charity and his unusual modesty. He also had unbelievable recall. But a great Byron story is rare and when, come to think of it, was the last time you heard a really good Nicklaus story?

Hogan rebuilt himself while Jack, when pressed, was able to reinvent himself. These are not even close. Five majors after having a head-on collision with a bus cannot be compared to crafting a new image. Different men, different eras, different experiences. Actually, I can think of one commendable Nicklaus story that survives on its own merit without Chi Chi Rodriguez's wit and self-deprecation in the telling. And, in the tradition of Hogan's alleged sixth lesson, Jack himself has either a) forgotten it; b) chooses not to recall it; or c) it never happened.

The provenance is a bit sturdier. It comes from Bill Sansing, one of Jack's early team in his Golden Bear ventures. I'm indebted to *Austin American-Statesman* golf writer Doug Smith who included it in an interview with Sansing years ago in his *Hill Country Golfer*. Sansing had accompanied Jack in 1980 to the Atlanta Classic where he opened with a uncharacteristic 78. Nicklaus emerged from the scorer's tent to a swarm of reporters. He stood there in the heat patiently answering questions "for what seemed like forever," Sansing recalled. "He was so polite with all of them. He was soaked in sweat and exhausted when he got to the locker room where some more reporters got him and went through the same questions. Again he was most patient.

"Halfway through the session in the locker room, he whispered to me to get us a private room that he needed to talk to me. He finished with the press and we went into this little room, not much more than a closet.

"We're all alone, nobody can hear us?" he asked.

"Yes," Sansing replied.

Jack then let out a scream that Sansing estimated lasted about 20 seconds. "He just had to let that out, and he wasn't going to do it in front of others." Jack rebounded with a cathartic 67 the next day. He still missed the cut, but the following week, let the record reflect, he won the U.S. Open and, later, that year's PGA Championship. I've asked Jack about this but he said he has no recollection of the incident.

The length of Hogan's shadow always brings to mind Smitty. He so savored attending the first Legends of Golf, the inspiration for the Senior PGA Tour, that he bought the Dumpster! Smitty paid $50 for its contents, thus coming to rightfully possess all sorts of ephemera: letters, a lifetime supply of day passes, parking badges, pairing sheets and programs—along with more unsavory and less desirable keepsakes. Smitty concedes that buying the trash was an unusual reaction to what was by all accounts a fabulous finish, but those commemorative Legends plates and caps on sale in the pro shop just didn't fill the bill.

"It's something you just do," he said with the matter-of-fact rationale of a daredevil assessing a stunt. Smitty may be certifiably eccentric; he's also the only man I know who would have followed Sam Snead into the men's room for an autograph. Stranger still, he got it, though the Slammer was not amused.

Smitty told me he often enjoyed the solitary pleasure of playing a few holes alone at dusk, that alluring time of day when the course is deserted and golf is its most absorbing. When he could he would play three balls. One ball he'd pretend would be his, one would be Byron Nelson's and one would be Ben Hogan's. Hogan, he told me laughing and shaking his head, always won, testament, I suppose, to his eternal place in the game's collective subconscious.

A footnote that might even impress Smitty concerns Harry Vardon, the immortal British champion who also enjoyed solitary practice sessions. He wrote of a friend who carried the charade of being two separate golfers beyond his imagination. Not only would the man play two balls, he would bring along an extra set of clubs, pretending to more completely simulate an opponent when he was, in fact, alone.

Obscured in Hogan's writings is a 1942 *Esquire* article on a subject that does not get sufficient attention, *When Golf is No Fun*. Given Hogan's focus, it's certainly an intriguing subject for him to tackle. This is, you understand, a man who late in life told *Golf Digest* that he played golf with friends, but that he didn't play friendly golf. A round with Hogan could be many things: mesmerizing, fascinating, intimidating, instructive, but how jovial could it have been? Then again, who better to plumb the game's depths?

Real fun—not the grind of defeat and defiance that drives a man to take solace in arranging his closets—must necessarily be fleeting for the pros who face uncertainty with every swing. Other than depositing a check, the fun hardly lasts longer than the instant between a disappearing putt and the calculations regarding the next drive. The most important shot is always next. Not that the pros can't be funny. I'm indebted to the tour player who once described his putting as having gotten so bad "he couldn't find water putting off a boat." Sarcastic, self-deprecating, wry, tormented, the gallows humor pays tribute to the heritage of personal suffering that buttresses the game like a Prestwick railroad tie. Telling? Yes, indeed—if not exactly evocative of fun *per se*. It was Harold Hilton, the winner of two British Opens and four British Amateurs, who when asked, late in life, if he hadn't fought the good fight, agreed: "Sometimes—when I could see the humour of it all." That is a most enlightened and unplugged attitude. The exceptional Mickey Wright was asked in 1991 whether she would say she was a competitive person on the golf course. "I must have been," she considered, "but I never felt competitive."

Hogan adopts a light and sympathetic tone in the article, offering advice to an amateur who has written to him about his flagging game.

"The first thing I'd honestly advise a fellow who is disgusted with his golf," Hogan recommends, "is to change the company he's playing in. If he changes to playing with fellows who enjoy themselves without worrying themselves and others about bad shots and high scores, he'll begin to relax at his game. He will get a better score because he won't be trying so desperately that he tightens up stiffer than a steel rail."

Often as not, he continues, it's fixating on non-golf distractions that makes the duffer a "nervous basket case," perhaps, "it was something he ate, the war, priorities, taxes or something else far away from a golf course" that is to blame for his indifferent play. Hogan's bullish on fifteen minutes (to two hours) of putting into a cup on the carpet each night. Given his notorious putting problems late in life, no less an expert than Bobby Locke, who many consider among the finest putters ever, surprisingly picked Hogan as the best. In the back of *Bobby Locke on Golf*, the author goes through the bag choosing the best contemporary player with each club. He selects Hogan, singling him out not for his ball striking, long irons or anything else, but for his putting.

"Golf is a very convenient thing for him to blame as the source of his unhappiness," Hogan concludes in *When Golf is No Fun*. "He should be happy he has golf handy for that alibi and relief."

Teammates of another old school figure, Ty Cobb, believed he would have been successful in any endeavor, "a great banker, a famous general, a successful industrialist—outstanding in any field he chose. No other man ever had his frenzy for excellence. Cobb's passion was to finish first in everything." The same is often said to have been true of Hogan.

In considering Hogan, sportswriter Al Laney wrote: "He does not give you the feeling of being in presence of a great artist, as Bob Jones did, but he does give you the feeling of being in the presence of a master craftsman." Certainly the artist and the craftsman would view many things differently, practice include, which speaks to the earlier disparity.

Aside from the personal traumas that drove men like Hogan or Cobb to glory, how grateful Hogan must've been to have golf as an alibi and a relief, as an outlet to express himself. Perhaps that was Hogan's real secret, to have discovered early in life a quest that so fully fed his strengths and appeased his weaknesses like no other.

a flick of the wrist

It was one of those tricks you assumed all caddies knew, akin to a fraternal handshake, or it came instinctually to those expected, in a crassly expressed and inaccurate job description, to "show up, keep up and shut up."

Just goes to show, it's not true! One informal barroom estimate placed the figure of those who loop for a living with the skill closer to only 10 or 20 percent. "You don't see guys do it a lot," says Mark Huber. A professional caddie for 20 years (18 years), most recently with Doug Tewell on the Champion's Tour, Mark credits boredom, disinterest in repeatedly bending over and the urge to entertain himself as motivations. Mark once played a lot of baseball and he suggests that time well spent in bullpens helped him hone his enthusiasm for tedium relief. It only reconfirms the bullpen as a source of scholarly enterprise, one of the great think tanks in sports. "I think I learned it through boredom," he says modestly or, lending credence to the original theory, "through osmosis."

As to the secret: "I really don't know what the trick is."

Overlooking the "strangest favor anyone's asked of me," Mark kindly offered to pass along the following exclusive hints to one of pro golf's great mysteries. How do they pick up a ball off the ground with a wedge?

Like most things in golf results should not be expected overnight. Artfully lifting balls from the green will require, Mark says, "probably a year" of practice. All of us who envy the nonchalance of the professional caddie, especially those who never quite mastered bouncing up a tennis ball from the ground, will find the process humbling if ultimately rewarding. Could an impressive casual display be worth a stroke or two before the start of a round? There's no telling, so let's get crackin'.

Mark likes to see the ball **positioned straight down the shaft**. He recommends pulling a sand wedge, a **sixty-degree** lofted club is best, the more offset on it the better. There are other methods; one, Mark notes, sets the toe (top edge) of the club behind the ball at the start of the move. While it may achieve the desired result, Mark prefers to work with the **ball closer to the hosel** (heel). Either is acceptable.

Grip way down the shaft touching the metal below the grip. Now with the edge of the club peeking underneath the ball, quickly roll your wrist employing a **very strong grip** (V's pointed to the right shoulder) scooping underneath the ball in a relaxed but decisive upwards flip. Plan on giving yourself a preliminary, set-up bounce similar to the set-up for a spike in volleyball. Get the ball up in the air then (someday soon with a flourish) under control, bounce it once. Pop it up to the desired height with that languid second bounce. You got it!

Practice the snapping thrust first without a ball, then work up to beginning sets of 10 reps, preferably with new balls. Acorns, stray pecans,

Courtesy: Mark Huber

Mark Huber

bits of tees on the ground provide a fun challenge; for indoors, Nerf items, folded socks or Wiffle golf balls also work well. Malted milk balls, spare change, caplets, small pieces of dried fruit—prunes, etc., dog toys, most office supplies and packing peanuts do not. (This paragraph is the author's own input. The great champion and teacher Tommy Armour had his students only hit brand new balls ceremoniously presented by assistants and teed to the proper height. Same thing in play here—there's a psychological boost. Just a personal preference: old 'water hole' balls or range balls won't get you anywhere.) Should you ever bump into a caddie by the name of *Whiz* you might discreetly catch the act of a man with Zorro-like dexterity, his blade doing everything from bouncing a ball through his legs, behind his back, everything just short of playing it off his nose before depositing it into a bib pocket. Tiger's no slouch either. Of course it goes without saying that the enhanced hand-eye coordination from practicing this trick will have a salutary effect on your overall game, especially in building up the wrists similar to the effort extended by the *Karate Kid* buffing cars. Hee ya!

tap it down

Those who find dexterity with a wedge child's play, welcome! Let me introduce you to the platinum standard of style points, the trick that separates the men sporting a deep tan with a one-iron in their bags from the *broccoli choppers* infesting pro shops on Saturday morning. Tapping a ball down on the tee is strictly tour material. Truly a risk and reward shot. *Have you got it in you?*

A master PGA teacher would have us visualize this move as a "**vertical tap**." A delicate maneuver to be sure, one that calls for clear focus and a steady hand. The two-handed tap, he adds, "is for weenies, **one hand is for dudes**." He recommends grip pressure identical to that for the pitch shot. As he did not add specifics, we're left to assume that it has much to do with the ancient *dictum* on squeezing the little bird. All together now: Not too much or we'll kill the bird, but not so loose or the thing flies off. Why we're holding a little bird, be it too tight or not tightly enough, has never been fully explained. Why shouldn't we let it go? How big a bird is it? What about the risk of avian flu? And what if the bird has ideas of its own, or starts pecking? Our anonymous pro adds that too much flex will cause one to "lose control," which leads us back, after all, to a **secure grip**.

A second top 100 Golf magazine teacher, also, for some reason, reluctant to lend his name, suggests a **45-degree shaft angle**. "That's going to put the sole of that club somewhere near 90 degrees or parallel to the ground," he suggests. "We've got to get that shaft angle just right so that club will work just like a hammer driving a nail into the ground." He also endorses the one-handed tap. "It's gotta be the one-handed tap or, without question, style points will be deducted."

Consensus among pro shop faithful centers on the hands being held slightly higher than they would be at address. This more vertical position also assists in flattening out the sole of the driver, which may in fact be slightly rounded depending upon make and model. The flatter the surface contacting the teed ball from above, obviously, the better.

"There is no real trick to tapping down a ball," offers a recent past president of his PGA section. "You just have to remember that you have to **hit it very lightly**." Let's give it a go.

Note: various soil types, especially those predominantly clay-based, common in southwestern and southern climes may present additional challenges. The tee must be secure in its mooring and upright with insertion depth a matter of preference. Experiment with the various high technology tee designs. The author has found limited success with the 2 ¾ inch extra long Zero Friction Tee. *Dudes*, however, may consider the three prongs an unfair advantage. Never mind. Accomplishing the move with two hands is no reason to be ashamed. Oversized drivers, it must be said, offer no clear advantage when compared to earlier generations of metal woods, or those of persimmon with brass sole-plates.

biofeedback training for bobby

It *was* slightly underhanded. Dr. Deborah Graham, a clinical psychologist was asked to render an opinion second-hand. What Deborah, who has long worked with golfers, did not know was that her test subject was no less than a young and struggling Robert T. Jones, Jr.

Graham lives in the Texas Hill Country hamlet of Boerne with a happy menagerie of formerly stray dogs, cats, a cockatiel or two, and husband Jon. She continues to work with numerous pro tourists—hundreds through the years—keeping in touch now mostly by phone. I'd listened to her presentation, read her book, sampled her methodology, and would occasionally run into her at tour events. Steps from the first tee at the Texas Open in nearby San Antonio, she'd be there to offer her clients a quick word of reassurance before their rounds.

The eradication of the slice notwithstanding, surely the hottest modern field remains the inner workings of the brain. There's certainly no shortage of explorers and practitioners: hypnotherapists, Buddhists, psychologists, psychiatrists, Samaritans, and shamans of good intention.

Deborah was an early entrant. LPGA players presented her with a fertile area of study for her dissertation. Her later successes would also have to include the persuasion to the benefits of therapy of a handful of grizzled male senior pros. She was also the first person I'd heard highlight the trials faced on the road by professional woman golfers. Perhaps no surprise in hindsight, these routinely had nothing to do with elements of the swing or intricacies of the short game. Golf is an ascetic quest for either sex, and things were then much more complicated for single women. The isolation could be acute. Deborah learned that in extreme situations the only conversation a female golfer might have in the course of a tournament day would be with her caddie. As was true for her male clients, golf problems were often ground in deep amidst trials and hurts unrelated to golf. As if the game weren't hard enough. The usual suspects: families, relationships, the weight of expectations, perceived slights, a veritable Pandora's shag bag both familiar to working men and women, and unique to a life spent following the sun. All these would ideally have to be peeled back and addressed. The infuriation of poor tournament play amounted to just one more piece of emotional baggage tossed on the pile. Whether it's the money list or monthly quotas, the bottom line remains a cruel measure. To hear a pro golfer—a he, in this case—as I once did, express his self-worth solely in terms of his place on the money list is just the sort of self-perpetuating trap that Deborah and other mental game experts seek to dispel. The fluctuating state of golf psychosis remains outside the scope of this book. It does seem to a layman, anyway, that despite so many "advances," the problems present a remarkably stable if not boom market (a telethon, perhaps?). We can wipe out golf anger in your lifetime. Your pledge dollars can make a difference.

Graham's work is "golf specific" but the bigger social issues uncovered in her research—it now seems obvious for all professional athletes, as the headlines attest—had been neglected, underappreciated or suppressed. There was also the machismo factor. Loners by nature, golfers were reticent to seek help—for anything—let alone to consult a "shrink," or share deeply personal concerns, least of all with a competitor. The stories are certainly heartwarming of touring pros helping each other out with just the right tip at the right moment. And then, there is fuel for the suspicious. The story is told of the leading player who liked to test out his swing theories—not on himself, oh no—but on unsuspecting competitors who came to him in their innocence seeking advice. Always quick with a tip was our 'good egg' who keenly watched the results. Such skillful deceit would bring approving nods from a Borgia!

Today golfers routinely and openly work in tandem with a bevy of well-being specialists. They wear amulets of precious metals and magnets with mysterious properties. The search for a competitive edge long ago supplanted any stigma regarding counseling. Coaches, whatever their actual discipline, who navigate the mental game, are often publicly credited. To her pleasant surprise, Deborah said the old goats were surprisingly receptive. "There were some, of course, who were a little bit leery because they were from what we tend to call the Old School, as in 'this is something I'm supposed to take care of myself.'

"Kind of in a joking way, we teased them, and said, 'Yes, you're losing distance and you're losing your vision, but you can gain what you're losing with your mental skills.' " That got their attention. She and Jon launched their company, GolfPsych. Her doctoral thesis was expanded into a book, *The Eight Traits of Championship Golfers*. It develops a personality profile based on the Cattell 16 Personality Factor questionnaire which she's applied and honed. Students now teach the eight traits across the globe.

"We've been able to quantify, label, identify, and create steps for learning and change to help more people do that," she says. "Champions have been thinking like champions forever."

Back to our case study. She received the following details save for Jones's identity:

- Male subject
- 24 years old
- Former child golf prodigy
- Had enjoyed considerable achievement in major championship play with periods of sporadic inconsistency and disappointment.

The golfer was described as being reserved and modest, highly intelligent and well educated. [It's easy to fall into this medical chart staccato pattern, excuse me.] Subject has also shown susceptibility and sensitivity to the strain of major tournament competition; eats faddishly and has routinely experienced dramatic weight loss during tournament week. All this was certainly true enough.

Jones entered the 1926 U.S. Open as the reigning British Open champion. To date he'd won two U.S. Amateurs, and a U.S. Open. Three times he'd finished tied for second in his national championship, losing once in a playoff. He'd also recorded two other top ten finishes. Some intriguing psychological back story... there was also his impetuous fury on his initial trip around the Old Course at St. Andrews. I'm not sure I mentioned that to Dr. Graham, nor his early penchant for club-throwing. His U.S. Amateur record also featured some disheartening episodes during what came to be called his seven lean years. Jones was cognizant of the criticism regarding his inability to capitalize, a difficult and (in many cases) self-fulfilling burden on those so highly touted. All that set up this startling admission, included in a treatise on short putts in the superlative *Bobby Jones on Golf.*

Jones wrote:

> *I shall never forget my feeling as I prepared to hole my last putt at Scioto, in Columbus, Ohio, to win the United States Open in 1926. The thing could not have been over three*

inches in length. Yet, as I stepped up to tap it in, the wildest thought struck me. "What if I should stub my putter into the turf and fail to move the ball?" I very carefully addressed the putt with my putter blade off the turf and half-topped the ball into the hole. Sounds a bit psycho, doesn't it?" But golfers can get that way.

In answer to your question, yes, sir, it does indeed sound a bit psycho. Not that you are the first golfer to entertain such morbid thoughts, or find yourself adrift on tension's debilitating tide.

Such moments may be more common and endemic than we realize. Greg Norman was in the enviable position of being a blissful five shots up and staring at a straight-forward-enough three-foot birdie putt on the 71st green at Turnberry in 1986. Oddly enough, he could not see this simplest of putts. He was, if you can imagine it, momentarily snow-blind. Caddie Pete Bender recalled the moment to author Norman Dabell in *Fourteen Clubs and the Old Claret Jug*. Norman turned to his man and said: "You know, Pete, I'm so damned nervous I can't see the line to the hole. You better tell me where to hit it and how hard." Give Norman points here for at least recognizing what was happening to him, and asking for help. Recognition, say those who mine the deep waters of golf consciousness seem to agree, is imperative to a resolution.

Pete told him. Shark, the caddie observed, was "hardly able to hold the putter." The resulting putt blew three feet past the hole but Norman was able to collect himself. He rammed home the come-backer to secure the win. Phew!

Dr. Graham offered the following analysis of Bobby's near-psychotic episode:

Sounds as though this young man is like one of many players we work with who is gifted with dueling mental strengths that can actually compromise his play. One strength being that he is very intelligent and analytical, the other being that he is a gifted and creative athlete. Left unchecked the analytical skill can win the internal competitive war by suppressing the athlete with excessive worry, rumination, doubt, analysis, tension and a very busy mind.

Like our clients with such dueling strengths, the internal battle during competition between the analytical mind and the athletic mind can become quite intense. [While some level of analysis is required to play your best, golf is actually much easier for players who are not excessively abstract and intelligent.]

(Author's note: Finally! A gleam of hope. Thank you, doctor! "Golf," The Edinburgh Evening Dispatch noted on May 1, 1891, "keeps the mind from being quite vacant; but the mind must be quite vacant for golf.")

In some people it becomes very difficult to turn off the analysis and rationalization—making it very difficult to access the great natural and trained athletic skills when they need them the most. We help these players reach peak performance by teaching them techniques for quieting their minds and relaxing their bodies—in a sense by teaching them to put themselves into a meditative state on cue. While we use many techniques like thought-stopping, various relaxation techniques, nutrition, etc., our most effective technique is a type of biofeedback training we have designed to both quiet the mind and relax the body, accomplishing the goal of freeing up the "athlete" and allowing the golfer to maximize his or her skills under all types of playing conditions. Without testing him, my guess is that this talented young man could benefit a great deal from some nutritional counseling and training to help quiet his mind and relax his body.

Bad news, Mr. Jones. You're going to have to back away from the peach pie, and forget about the ice cream. In all seriousness, Jones was by all accounts 'a good eater.' His diet would improve with maturity (as presumably has Tiger's), concern about his weight and the realization that *chowing* down was perhaps not the best preparation for six straight days of 36 holes of high-wire tension match play. (In *Down the Fairway* Jones notes losing 18 pounds during the U.S. Amateur in August, 1919; 12 pounds in three days during the 1925 U.S. Open—both, incidentally, resulted in tough losses.) Given the enormous mental strain that enveloped Jones, duly referenced by his numerous biographers, it's no wonder that at times he could hardly get down anything more substantial than a piece of toast or a sandwich. Still, he seemed to do all right, notwithstanding the occasional vengeful sprites dancing around his head over three-inch putts.

We should remind ourselves that Jones *made* his putt. All the great ones do *when they have to*. It's a rogue's gallery of those who could not sink what to the uninitiated appears to be the easiest of putts. Perhaps one year there could be an 'almost-champions' dinner to wash away those draining failures from the Masters. That's the thing about the great ones, they get it done. Paul Runyan distilled that essence down to eleven words, as true today as they have been or ever will be in divining the great from the very good. "A champion," he observed, "is as good as he has to be." So it is. The immortals seem to have an extra gear, an as-yet undetected synapse that regulates exactly how much is needed, how much can be expended, how much is left in the tank. Would it be unsympathetic to the scientific method, and the good doctor Graham, to think that at the end of the day there must also be something else at work? Some monumental good luck or, as Harvey Penick, a psychologist of a different pedigree and vintage, believed that when someone won it was simply their time?

draw a breath

> Q: In the final analysis, who beats the golfer?
> A: The golfer. [laughs] Most of the time, the golfer—
> regardless of their ability.
> —Harry Cooper

They all say it. The one essential to an effective pre-shot routine is to first take a deep diaphragmatic breath. When we're scared our breathing becomes strained. When less oxygen enters the brain, the mind races, the body tenses. We become agitated. We try too hard. Tension and adrenalin spell ruination for a movement so reliant on timing and as physically awkward as the golf swing, let alone an action as involved as a meaningful putt. An asset in other more reactive sports, in golf, the rush is a liability. The root of nearly every problem in golf, short of an act of God, is simply: too much tension.

The so-called self-imposed "fight or flight" response is said to be a vestige from our stalking prey and avoiding becoming some other predator's dinner. What, after all, is *choking* but a heightened state of anxiety, an inability to respond to unusual circumstances or the weight of expectations? It may indeed be a literal explanation of what's taking place. The Mayo Clinic is studying these weighty matters in probing the 'yips.' We're told that fluctuations in breathing induce (don't get excited—oops, too late) arousal, and in golf we don't want too much of that.

If enough of the good stuff does not reach the brain, we have to work harder. We become flustered. We rush. Our performance is imperiled. Tragic, but there it is. Here again it's not hard to find examples. Golf at all levels is positively littered with them. Greg Norman's final nine holes in the '96 Masters were a classic example, a toxic miasma of high-tension torment, over-excitement, discomfort and plain, unadulterated fear. Sure, there were technically—imperfect swings, bad decisions, uncommitted swings. A better explanation is that he lost it; a winner of 75 professional tournaments absolutely lost his natural frame of reference and his fluid swing was gone. Don't talk about muscle memory. If it were just up to the muscles, the pros would never miss a green. It had nothing to do with the elements of his golf swing, the grip, the swing plane. Doubt undermined him. What must his pulse rate have been during that fateful unraveling? Off the charts, surely. That ghastly chop of a tee shot he made at the 16th hole and his fitful swipe at cleaning the mud off the club in disgust were almost too much to bear. Worse, it all looked familiar.

It reminds me of a story from a college golf coach who was asked to pull the van over on the way to a tournament. He figured one of his players was car sick. It wasn't that at all. The player had merely become so uncomfortable riding in the back next to a course-load-full of white out of bounds stakes that he just couldn't take it anymore. The coach understood, and the seating was adjusted. Not surprisingly, no one else wanted to switch seats and be forced to stare at the ghastly stakes.

Jesper Parnevik stood awaiting the start of his singles match, trying hard not to take notice of his surroundings. "I could hardly breathe on the first tee," he recalled, no doubt accurately, for the first tee of a Ryder Cup is a place where little oxygen circulates, "because I really didn't know where the ball was going." That would do it. That, and his opponent over there loosening up, some chap named Woods.

Parnevik's triumph in halving the Brookline match demonstrates that the problems are not insurmountable. The stomach butterflies, or as Nicklaus said famously, can be assembled to fly in formation. Perhaps the most decisive step is recognition, awareness. Every golfer in hindsight realizes that it takes very little to trigger anxiety. The utterance of three harmless little words can prompt a damaging outbreak: "We need this" or "Knock it in." The words should be stricken from use on the golf course.

Gay Hendricks happened to be watching Tiger on television when he nearly jumped out of his chair. The Colorado-based psychologist is the author of a staple on of breath work, *Conscious Breathing*. He noticed Tiger "shift into that deeper breathing before he hits the ball, and always he hits the ball after the out breath. So he doesn't try and hit the ball as he's taking in a breath. He hits it on the out breath." Gay's book, *Conscious Golf*, discusses this in some detail.

No less than Sir Henry Cotton seconds the tip. In *Play Better Golf* he refers to this as one of his "pegs," a redoubtable key acquired over a lifetime to which he felt he could always return. "Breathe out completely before striking. This is always worth remembering…. It works for putting, too." It will only work though if you can remember to do it, as Annika Sorenstam was able to in awaiting her first momentous tee shot playing with the men at Colonial.

Several years ago, it was my good fortune to be in the back of the room when Tom Jenkins was giving a talk to a group of pedigreed junior golfers. Hardly a household name, Tom's done very well for himself on the Champion's Tour, and he gave a thoughtful and articulate talk. The journeymen players can be so much more pleasant and candid.

"I still get nervous," he assured us. "I want to feel nervous as many times as I can. That means I'm there. That means I'm doing my job. That's what you want. That's what you want, to desire, to have. You should love that feeling. That's what it's about." He not only expected to get nervous, he said, in fact he looked forward to it. That recognition allowed him to embrace the feelings, turning them into a positive. No wonder winners are said to be a different breed of cat.

Bernard Darwin considered the importance of breathing but the following maxim, equal parts clinical and poetic, is perhaps symptomatic of someone frequently, we gather, at war with his own malevolent golf demons:

> One important thing is not to take a deep breath at the top of the swing and come down on the ball with too violent a burst of melody. Another is not to stop as we reach the ball but to finish, of course in a chaste and classical attitude, with the music still flowing evenly from our lips.

It's said about hydration that apparently by the time we get thirsty it's too late. So it often is with recognition of our own emotional state, of which we may be wholly unaware. The pros *get it*, they know adrenalin is inevitable and potentially hazardous, particularly on the greens, particularly when it matters most. During the 1999 Masters, when the questions about '96 still politely lingered, Norman talked about the role of his longtime caddie, Tony Navarro. "His job is to try to calm down his boss. . . .He just wants to calm you down and get you back into the position where you should be, with a clear head and a clear mind and a clear approach to what you want to do." J.H. Taylor, the great early twentieth century British champion, said it was "by concentration of thought upon the business at hand [that] I am enabled to conquer that feeling of nervousness and to finally wear it down." No wonder these guys rarely smile.

The time pros spend checking and re-checking the line on critical putts often cloaks their primary intent. This has been true for about forever. They can read the greens. Their caddies know the greens. What the putt will do is not so much a mystery. What they are really doing—or attempting—like boxers dancing to clear their heads—is trying to get their breath under control and calm themselves. At their best, they refuse to hit a shot until they're ready, though it's worth pointing out that were this true of amateur golfers, we might never finish.

Bob Jones had the presence of mind to notice:

> *I had been putting quickly while my breath was coming in short gasps and my ears ringing as I leaned over the ball.... I resolved that no matter how much time I consumed, I was going to tranquilize my breathing before I made another putt. So I began to take great pains to study the line. I really did not study the line, for I have never been able to see more rolls and bumps in a minute than I could in five seconds, but I was giving my breathing a chance to quiet down. You have no idea what a steadying effect upon the nerves can be had by doing*

> *some little thing in a natural manner. Light a cigarette, pick*
> *up a twig, or anything to take up a little time.*

So many great golfers have found relief in smoking that, despite the health risk and the inevitable litter, one might do worse for his golf than consider taking up a pack of regular Camels. Just kidding. It is hard to dismiss it outright. The smoking side in a team event would be exceptional in eternal competition: Vardon, Jones, Hogan, Palmer, Daly. Who else? Bobby Locke, irascible on many subjects, was the rare smoker who disagreed on its intrinsic competitive value.

"I smoke about five cigarettes a day," he allowed, "and never smoke when I am playing golf. I find smoking upsets my concentration, but more important it gives my opponent too many clues as to what my inner reactions are." A keen observer of human nature, he adds that "If an opponent was playing well, he'd be smoking one cigarette every three holes. But when I had them on the run it was three cigarettes a hole. When I saw them chain-smoking, I said to myself, 'Keep up the pressure and you will be all right.'

On the issue of artificial stimulants, it will be interesting to see what the future holds. Several years ago hall of famer Nick Price expressed his qualms regarding suspected use of Beta Blockers on the PGA Tour. An unapologetic critic of terrapine play, surprisingly his challenge elicited—excuse the expression—barely a murmur. New generations of high blood pressure medications that successfully block adrenalin and prevent wild heart beat fluctuations would have to be a temptation given the huge sums at stake. Like other athletes constantly searching for an edge, professional golfers are only human.

To the anxious golfer, anything must be considered an improvement over simply standing and stewing in one's own mental juices. Laura Davies, a fast player, was once observed waiting for the green to clear before playing her second shot on a tightly wooded par-five. She paced like a caged animal. Fred Couples reportedly amuses himself by counting leaves on the trees. Nick Faldo's former caddie, Fanny Sunesson once successfully diluted major championship pressure by engaging her boss in an absorbing room-by-room discussion of the construction of his new home. Scheherazade, it seems, would have made a terrific caddie.

A remarkable individual, the Vietnamese monk and author Thich Nhat Hanh offers an exceptional safety valve tailor-made for golfers, a walking meditation detailed in his book *Peace is Every Step*. An opportunity to, as they say, stay in the present, he counsels awareness in each slow mindful step by coordinating our breathing.

> For example, we may take three steps with each in-breath and three steps with each out-breath. So we can say, "In, in, in. Out, out, out." "In" is to help us to identify the in-breath. ...If your lungs want four steps instead of three, please give them four steps. If they want only two steps, give them two. The lengths of your in-breath and out-breath do not have to be the same. ...If you feel happy, peaceful, and joyful while you are walking, you are practicing correctly.

golf and chew gum *

Regular readers of *Psychopharmacology* magazine are well aware (What's that? You let your subscription lag?) of the extensive ongoing research related to the efficacy of such novel modern "delivery systems" as nicotine patches, gums, sprays, and inhalers. Of related interest to those who haven't been keeping up, there is also: *A naturalistic investigation of the effects of day-long consumption of team, coffee and water on alertness, sleep onset and sleep quality*. And who could hardly put down: *Effects of the non-competitive NMDA-receptor antagonist memantine on morphine—and cocaine-induced potentiation of lateral hypothalamic brain stimulation reward?*

Light reading is fine but the golfer in search of immediate game enhancement could do far worse than spending some quality time considering the findings of cognitive specialist Professor Andrew B. Scholey and his colleagues in the Human Cognitive Neuroscience Unit at the University of Northumbria in Newcastle, England. An increased understanding of the relationship between glucose administration, heart rate and cognitive performance is just one of their recent intriguing avenues of study. What does this have to do with us?

Two words: chewing gum.

Fomented understandably for years by the chewing gum industry, there may in fact be something to this. For instance, according to the chirpy *Great American Chewing Gum Book*, chewing serves as a "sublimation of the fidgets, an outlet for nervous energy…to ease tense nerves and muscles." OK, no one is developing sublimating the fidget methodology, not as yet. That would be pushing it. There are some encouraging results, however, Dr. Scholey's among them, that demonstrate chewing gum enhances memory. Yes. "The participants who chewed performed better in tests and working memory," he concludes. Why this is so is quite complicated and involves parts of the brain with which you've likely never concerned yourself. Basically, chomping makes the mouth water. This in turn convinces the glands into expecting food, which in turn causes them to release a surge of insulin. When more oxygen and more glucose, what Scholey refers to as "brain food," reaches the brain we "learn better."

According to Scholey: "One interesting thing we saw in our study was that chewing increased heart rate. Anything," he told NewScientist.com, "that improves delivery of things like oxygen in the brain, such as an increased heart rate, is a potential cognitive enhancer to some degree."

Let's not overlook whiter teeth, fresher breath, a great smile with a reduced cigarette craving for additional positives. Back to golf, my own suspicion is that, regardless of what chewing does to the insulin receptors in the hippocampus—yes, the hippocampus—it serves as a distraction, in a good way; chewing, like mindlessly working one's way through a bag of pumpkin seeds, gives us something to do rather than fall prey to the destructive whims of lurking pessimism.

In one study, mastication released 17 percent more oxygen. Seventeen more percent! Scholey's 2002 study found gum-chewers scored nearly 25 percent better on a battery of memory and attention tests, such as immediate and delayed word recall. Could that translate into strokes? Hard to say.

Now it could be suggested that memory to a golfer is a mixed blessing, or worse. No less than the aforementioned senior golfer Tom Jenkins once told *USA Today*'s Jerry Potter: "You've got to forget what you did yesterday." After a bad round he'll leave the golf course, "go home and forget about it." Score another difference for the pros if in fact they are able to leave their work at the office. Jim Thorpe had a slightly different take on it: "We don't do a lot of thinking out there. If you start thinking, you start making mistakes."

Skeptics may question the value in an increased heart rate. What about fight or flight? Without any direct chewing/golf context-dependent effect and arousal mechanism studies, let me just say this about that: it's at least plausible that chewing, proven to increase oxygen supplies to the brain, might help us think more clearly, providing that needed awareness to stave off fight or flight.

Bubblicious, Bazooka Blast Cherry, Wrigley Spearmint, Carefree, Xylitol, Chiclets, Chlorets, Dentyne Fire, Ice Arctic Chill or Ice Peppermint—it doesn't matter what brand or what flavor you chew, although research suggests it's best if it has a flavor. We don't yet know precisely why. One synopsis notes "…two crossover studies…report modulation of attentional performance by chewing gum, including improved performance in latter stages of a sustained attention task in the group who chewed flavored gum…The reasons for these differences are unknown…"

Let's not get carried away, there are a lot of variables to consider, including even the gum's composition. Anyone who recalls working over whatever that was that came with a pack of baseball cards can appreciate this last point. Certainly more research is needed. We await the findings and subsequent confirmation, for instance, from studies like: *Effects of gum hardness on the response of common carotid blood flow volume, oxygen uptake, heart rate and blood pressure to gum-chewing*. Incidentally, those of you who have let your subscription to the *Journal of Mastication and Health Sciences* lapse might find it prudent to re-subscribe.

* The preceding section was written while chewing several pieces of Peelu Fresh Spearmint Flavor Dental Chewing Gum, "The Cleansing Toothbrush Gum in the 100-piece economy size."

fellow competitors

Pairings matter. A good pairing can be serendipitous. It was Zach Johnson's good fortune to spend the final round of the 2007 Masters in the company of Vaughn Taylor. Same age, similar interests, similar "mellow" temperament, best buds since making their way through the mini-tours. "We enjoy each other's company," Johnson said shortly after receiving the green jacket. Who better to spend a pressure-packed afternoon in contention with at a major championship? Was it a factor? "Having a buddy next to you certainly doesn't hurt," he said. "He (Taylor) said some really nice, kind things and gave me support as well. In that respect, sure."

Of course they do. Who we play with makes a difference and, comforting thought, to varying degrees the same holds true for the pros. Tour players have no control over this, of course. Their scores call the tune. One must be ready to play one's best regardless of having drawn Bambi or Godzilla for the day. Same with us who show up to take pot luck putting our name on "the list". The pros, however, never have to suffer through cart-pooling, sharing close personal space akin to a seat in steerage for five hours with a stranger or, excuse me, an a-hole. They also have the additional insurance of a caddie for company and at their service; someone presumably with whom they get along, or at least for the money is willing to expend considerable effort on their behalf. A large part of that effort will entail controlling crowds or otherwise insulating their golfer from the unpleasant and distracting, a considerable luxury.

The best players enjoy other advantages: more favorable tee times for a start. There's also a big, supportive gallery, good for the ego. Pairings are more familiar, more predictable, in turn, fewer surprises. The winners start their week with the winners, part of a strictly defined hierarchy. Difficult to join the club, it recalls an old player maxim that conveys the catch-22 conundrum of life on tour: "Stay in Motel 6, play like Motel 6."

Top players also benefit at the gallery's expense. Tommy Bolt long ago noted the value of what he called "a nice deep human fence lining both sides of the fairway." He figured it could be worth a stroke or two which is significant. A large crowd, too, creates a kind of constant, anonymous, even inspirational, buzz while the movements and sounds from a few odd stragglers have a way of standing out as an annoyance.

It also holds that we, them—all of us—play better when we play with friends. This is an adjunct to an old and lovely observation attributed to Peter Thomson who believed "we play better when we play happy." Stands to reason, but what about the fire-and-brimstone types? The ones who first have to implode before their games catch fire? Or those who seem to clear the air with their tantrums? I'm not sure. From a safe distance the tempestuous Hale Irwin was once spotted vigorously chewing himself out under a stand of live oaks. Tied for the lead he'd just four-putted from about 12 feet early in the final round. He threw off enough vitriol for a *Psycho* screen test. Much to everyone's amazement, including his own, he went on to win that same afternoon. The tantrum had left him seemingly at peace, in a sort of private blissful daze. Hale had gone to that happy place, I suppose, perhaps sharing the contentment that apparently exists among murderers whose anger is dissipated with the one violent act that accomplishes their vendetta and relieves their anger.

"What's wrong with being in your own little world?" Blackie Sherrod rhetorically once asked in *The Dallas Morning News*. "They know me there."

Years ago, akin to the Thomson remark, I got wind of another view from the sunny side of golf. A dozen top tour players were serveyed for their best advice. Johnny Miller responded with "Play happy," which he attributed to Nancy Lopez's father, Domingo. Lanny Wadkins, once speaking of pairings during his ill-fated but otherwise exemplary broad-casting career, suggested an important corollary when he noted that: "It makes you feel confident when someone does things the same speed as you do." Pace of play doesn't get nearly the consideration with respect to its effect on performance as it warrants. Laura Davies was just one more example of a fast player positively unraveled by impatience, as she was repeatedly in a losing Solheim Cup effort. It may be the most prevalent, if no longer the most subtle, form of gamesmanship. Long after their play-ing days were through, Babe Ruth and Ty Cobb were playing what proved to be an aborted series of golf charity matches. Cobb was painfully metic-ulous, Ruth antsy and volatile. Things were not going well. The Babe spoke for millions of discouraged golfers when he mentioned that he could actually feel himself aging while *The Georgia Peach* lined up his putts.

I know of one death that may be attributed to slow play. It happened on the 18th tee while I was on the 10th. My group had teed off. I was walking and was joined by a couple with a cart; he played, she rode along. As we were leaving the tee someone came running down the adjoining 18th fairway calling for a doctor. There's no way of knowing whether it would have made any difference but the golfer in the cart insisted on first playing his way down to the hole rather than postpone the game. His female companion, you see, was a nurse. He refused to let her take the cart despite her repeated pleas. It was a hot, typical mid-summer afternoon in Texas. The deceased had been part of an early morning senior tournament. He died on the 18th tee. One hole to go. Would he have made it back to the clubhouse had the pace of play allowed him to earlier finish his round?

His body remained on the course for hours as by law, until the coroner's arrival, the corpse could not be removed. Someone rode out from the pro shop to ask that we play around the deceased, arresting swing thought though the sight presented—he'd been covered by a bag. Later an ambulance was seen cruising down the fairway, an incongruous reminder of what fate has in store. The shameless conduct of my playing partner went unremarked but I suspect he heard about it later. The obits were checked for the official cause of death during the next several days but, regardless of the medical explanation it was nothing other than gross negligence, first and foremost death by slow play.

Pace of play is such a discouraging topic. My home course annually hosts five divisions of state high school championships and officials have become inured to five and six-hour rounds. One old pro believed another whole generation of good golfers, though still just teenagers, had been lost. Only with a fresh start, he believes, inoculating the youngest entering the game, is there any hope of reversing the trend.

Revolutionary as it sounds, wouldn't tour life—and golf, generally—be much easier on everyone if, rather than go by score alone, the "turtles" were paired with the "turtles" and the "rabbits" played with the "rabbits?" The lesson of slow play's ravages might then be learned. The PGA Tour's rabbits would comfortably finish their rounds. They would eat dinner at a normal hour and be assured of a decent full night's sleep. The slugs could torment each other, forced to return to the golf course at dawn to try and get their rounds on time. Is it too much to ask that the highest levels of the game set a basic example of consideration? The answer is simple. Two champions noted for their fast pace, Nick Price and George Duncan had the same advice, over a half-century apart. Fine 'em!

"It is time that an example was made of someone," wrote Duncan, "however, whether he be American, British, or any other nationality. …Some golfers can dream themselves out of victory. Get on with it."

The National Golf Foundation often cites what it identifies as the 'intimidation factor' in explaining the early exodus of beginners from golf. There's no mystery. Those who know they don't know their way around sense they are unwelcome. They feel that pervasive air of condemnation from those who do know. Carry a bag of clubs into the pro shop and you'd just as soon walked into a photo session with the president wearing flip-flops. No one wants to feel inadequate. Little do beginners realize that golf's buttressed by inadequacy. Not that that's a bad thing. Were it easy, golf would never have made it out of the 1400s. It's no coincidence that the game's rise parallels the development of single malt Scotch. You can look it up.

So many humiliating layers. So many things one is expected to know. These only intensify over time. As they say, the better one plays the harder the game becomes. There is a perverse pleasure in knowing the pros share different if just as vexing anxieties. One young pro confessed feeling uneasy—this very early in his PGA Tour career—just knowing that a luminary (as it happened, Ben Crenshaw) was playing in the group directly behind him at Riviera.

A good pairing can be serendipitous.

In the 2005 B.C. Open, Ryan Palmer and Jason Bohn, frequent practice partners found themselves paired on the final day. Both were very much in contention. Palmer had a chance to win the tournament on the final hole. He missed his 14-footer. Bohn then coolly sank his 7-foot par putt for his first victory. Ryan Palmer shot 67-67 on the weekend only to lose to Bohn's two 66s.

"It's hard. You want him to do well," he said speaking of Bohn, but "you obviously want to win." He went on to say afterwards that their good play was infectious. They "started feeding off each other," he said. (If only there was a pay-out to the media for every time a tour player said this.)

The newly-crowned champion put the pairing in perspective.

"We kept each other loose," Bohn told John Kekis of the Associated Press. "I give a lot of credit to him. He kind of kept me loose out there. That was a big advantage for me."

Sure it was. Can we agree that had Bohn been playing with someone else, someone he didn't know, or didn't like, or someone bound to intimidate a tour newbie, a premier player like Tiger or ViJay, doing so without any especial effort, that the dynamic on the final day would have been different? At the very least, what Bohn clearly believed was an advantage —playing alongside his pal—would not have existed. In an earlier era, Tony Manero was said to have clearly benefited over the final holes at Baltusrol from the stewardship of Gene Sarazen during the 1936 U.S. Open. Complaints were in fact lodged though this was in the days before score alone, the more appropriate method, dictated pairings.

Bob Rifke had a good feeling. Justin Leonard's caddie had just spied the pairings for the final round of the British Open at Troon in 1997. Justin, five shots off the lead starting the day in third place, would be playing with everybody's favorite, the easy going Fred Couples.

"Justin loves and respects him and he was just a great partner to have on a day like that," Rifke told Norman Dabell. "It was a real laid-back day. I know it's the British Open final round but, believe me, it was just like playing a practice round. No matter whether Fred's leading or if he's in 40th place, his temperament's going to be pretty much the same. His caddie Joe and I are good friends, all four of us are good friends. So it was just a great, great pairing."

That's a dream pairing. No surprises. No distractions, no shenanigans, nothing to have to keep an eye on or out for. No problems with pace of play, or gamesmanship. Just golf. Given all the inherent uncertainties, Leonard could walk to the first tee knowing the circumstances for making a run couldn't be better. A propitious pairing hardly assures a win but it was something to build upon. Justin did, as indeed Manero still had to fulfill his destiny by shooting his final-round 67, over and above Sarazen's best intentions.

Sergio Garcia has been quick to acknowledge that he plays better when he's playing with people he likes. It's an admission that should come as no surprise to anyone who's followed his dramatic play, especially in the Ryder Cup. Ashling O'Connor, writing in *The Times*, on July 16, 2005, noted Sergio was paired with his Ryder Cup teammate Paul McGinley, "with whom he could share a morale-boosting high five if the mood demanded it." Lord knows, that would not have been the case were he playing with someone less amused or accustomed to Sergio's exuberance. He's not going to get a high or a low-five from _____ (name of American Ryder Cup team member). That brings to mind an old saw about the difference between the European and U.S. PGA tours; perhaps this has changed with globalization, they obviously see a lot more of each other these days. At night on the Euro Tour, it was said there'd be one table in the restaurant and twenty chairs. In the U.S., there'd be twenty tables with each player dining alone. Were there even a grain of truth to this over-simplification would it help explain the apparent lack of unity on recent American Ryder Cup teams? Quarterbacks invite their receivers to practice and 'hang out' during the off-season. Can bonding among golfers be that difficult?

> Q: Do you think it's easier to play better when everyone in your group is playing better, too. Do you feed off each other, or don't you believe in that?

Darren Clarke: It's always easier whenever all of the guys in the group are playing well. You know, you see good shots go into the greens all the time and that makes it a lot easier to do the same yourself.

David Cook, a past president of the National Sport Psychology Academy, has worked with many professional and collegiate athletes, golfers included. An exceptional presenter with a touch of down-home preacher in him, he's not averse to comforting an audience perhaps jittery at the prospect of delving into deep water. He'll say things like, "There's no mysticism, no guru stuff pulled out of the air. I'm coming at you as an engineer, coming at you with psychology, and we're going to put some feet on this thing."

He counsels his players, if need be, to imagine themselves as another player, someone they admire; no one else has to know. He tells of a client who (this some years ago) chose Curtis Strange as his imaginary player. Dr. Cook's powers of suggestion are reminiscent of a comment Michael Campbell made following his U.S. Open victory. The win followed an uninspired run of undistinguished, uneven, even awful, play; he'd begun the year missing five straight cuts. Campbell said he'd been so discouraged he was on the verge of quitting. He was asked an exceptional question: How was he able to "manufacture that sense of confidence" when he hadn't played well? Campbell's response was heartening, and I believe Dr. Cook would find it illustrative in counseling us about the answer to the question: which comes first—confidence or good shots.

"Pretend, just make believe," Campbell explained. "You just lie to yourself that you have confidence, and self-confidence takes over and believes that after a while, simple as that." Others have said the same about the creative process.

Lie to yourself? Simple as that? That's *ALL*? That's *IT*? @!%#$&!

secrets! get your secrets!

Indiana Jones stands before the ancient Crusader. Time is running out. Before him are dusty shelves. On one sits the true Holy Grail, the others are fakes. He must choose and choose wisely. It's a bit like that, really. Golf either has one secret, many secrets, or, perhaps, none at all, or far more than we can ever hope to comprehend. Some work instantly, some for a time but not until later, others only materialize through painstaking effort, while an unknown percentage are absolutely pointless. How to tell? I've no earthly idea.

In any event, we can't have a golf book without golf secrets. Here's a few to get you started:

Stay down, face the ball, complete the backswing, stay within your-self, keep your eye on the ball, breathe, finish high and watch it fly, the hands lead the club, grip down several inches, swing the clubhead, pull down, swing through, feel tall, play the ball off the "high" foot, use an "open" stance, waggle, don't "groove" your waggle, visualize, develop patience, place 60 percent of your weight on your left leg, cavity-backed, a stroke is not a jab, raise your left shoulder a little more than usual, "hook" away from trouble, move the ball back in your stance, balance, flex the knees, timing is everything, graphite, rotate and release, shake hands with the club, open your eyes, the first impression is the best, delay the hit, play within yourself, swing as hard as you can, "courageous timid-ity," keep your head down, stand tall like a matador, keep an eye out for the "lions" in the rough, close the face and hit down sharply, hit it hard, extend your arms through the ball, focus on what you can control.

Don't try and thank me, it's just part of the service. Collect and trade them with your friends!

more "secrets:"

I said to Ty Cobb, "What do you do to hit that ball so accurate?"

He said, "I have a loaded bat and I keep it in my room and I swing it at night and morning so that I can have the rhythm." Oh, right away I got in my mind, I said, "Oh, boy, I'm going to get a club and make it 22 ounces and put the right grip, reminder grip, and everything and swing it back and forth fifty times a day." And I did that. Inside a year and a half I had the perfect grip. I had the same grip that Hagen and Jones had. I used to be a terrible hooker and that ironed the hooker out.—Gene Sarazen

The secret of the golf game is the control of the tension of the fingers during the stroke. You can look anywhere else you like, and people always do, but the fact remains that golf is a game of hands, touch, control, or whatever else you like to call it; and in the end it is the gripping of the club which gives every golfer his category, sorting the wheat from the chaff. —Henry Cotton

Even his bad shots are good. That's the secret of golf. —Johnny Miller on Fred Couples

If there is a secret to golf, it is to know one's capabilities. —Cary Middlecoff

Golf is a business, and you have to approach it that way. You have to give careful thought to every shot. Every shot sets up what you are going to do next. Every shot has to be placed correctly. Don't ever just hit a shot without thinking it through. —Ben Hogan

There is no such secret—that's the secret.—Bob Duval

The secret of good golf is the employment of the visual image or mental picture.—Jack Heise

Strength is not the secret.—Jimmy Thompson

Water. Drink water.—Hollis Stacy

The secret is you have to exercise hard for longevity for a long life, happy life and productivity. But it is no use exercising if you don't eat correctly. —Gary Player

The best way to win any important event is to play just as one would play a private round at home, and not endeavor to accomplish the performance of a lifetime. There is such a thing as trying too hard; it begets anxiety, which is usually fatal— especially in putting.—Harry Vardon

The Secret is the correct functioning of the right leg, with emphasis on maintaining the angle of the right knee on the back and forward swings. Combined with a slight cupping of the left wrist, it produces optimum balance and control, and allows you to apply as much speed and power as you wish. —Jody Vasquez

It's a game of constant adjustment and the guy that adjusts the best, is the best player. And you ask any of the great players, they'll tell you, they have a couple of things they're thinking about any given day or week that works for them. You can call them gimmicks if you want, but I think they, the good players, stick to basic ideas and use those basics on a rotating basis. —Gene Littler

The best single piece of advice I could give any man starting out for a round of golf would be "take your time," not in studying the ground, and lining up the shot, but in swinging the club. —Bobby Jones

Come breakfast on Wednesday, the team's eating habits were making themselves known. We had sent somebody out to get olive oil for Mechanico (Miguel Angel Jimenez), because he was rather partial to a cereal bowl of boiled eggs swimming in a one-inch pool of the stuff. There was a contented look on his face as he tucked in. —Mark James

Probably the most important single thing is to feel that you are going to hole the putt, then stroke the ball the right way. —Walter Hagen

The best advice to all golfers is to play the game for the fun of the thing; take your defeats cheerfully and your victories with modesty. —H.G. Whigham

The secret is to take the club away from the ball slowly on a line almost parallel with the ground. Do it deliberately. —Arnold Palmer

A player must learn to slide the club in the palm and fingers of the right hand, on the upward swing, before he can successfully attain a correct golfing swing. …This is the great secret of a golfing swing, one which a boy, when learning picks up instinctively. It is a species of natural golfing touch, more than difficult to acquire when a golfer takes up the game in later years. Practice it; it is worth practicing. —Harold Hilton

Rhythm, my boy, unbroken rhythm—legs, arms, and body moving as one. —Archie Compston

If there is a secret to the game of golf, it's not what you do, it's how you do it. Because no matter what we do, whether we do it slow or fast, muscles and joints have to be at ease in their movements. —Bill Mehlhorn

stand please!

The large grandstand behind the 12th hole at the Masters emits a strong magnetism. Few patrons bother to walk back into the woods where the 11th hole, *White Dogwood*, begins. It is an especially pleasant spot at Augusta National, which is saying something. The tee is never crowded and the gathering often collegial. Far enough out of the way, one has to want to be there as only one shot can be seen, the drive. Tee shots quickly rise up and out of the glen and can't be followed.

One year a heralded player annually pegged as a sentimental favorite uncharacteristically turned in a peevish rage on the small group seated behind the 11th tee.

The player quickly stepped up and pounded his drive. It took off like a shot. As far as we knew it was fine. There must've been a squeak, however, barely audible to all but the player's finely-tuned rabbit ears. I happened to be directly behind him and I never heard it. If there was a noise it was likely committed by someone shifting in one of those plastic collapsible chairs that come with its own shoulder bag. They often squeak. The player spun in a rage, believing the offending click had instead come from a camera. A maddening distraction, cameras are perhaps only rivaled on tour by the invidious cell phone. With vigor he proceeded to verbally skewer the eight elderly seated spectators who, until then, had been placidly enjoying their day at the Masters. For sheer Vesuvian eruption value, nothing comes close in my experience save the time the head master entered sixth-grade study hall and with one swift kick shattered the knock-hockey set several boys had made. That historic event was replayed endlessly to our delight by an enterprising student who captured it all on a portable tape recorder.

"Was it YOU?!" the golfer demanded accusingly pointing a finger. "Or YOU?!" It was on the tip of my tongue to point out what had probably happened. There was no smoking camera. I kept my mouth shut, though, for fear of jeopardizing my credential or having a club shoved down my throat. "David" (not his real name) stomped off after his caddie leaving behind a vapor trail of rage and a dumbstruck group of startled patrons.

The unfortunate episode was another reminder of the fast-flowing undercurrent of player passion. Scratch beneath the calm exterior of even one of the more thoughtful and respected players and there's just another quiet man, one more tightly-wound thoroughbred ready to bust from his stall.

The major championship tantrum recalls a calculation that must haunt the pros contemplating their limited chances in the four big events. Driving home from the 1969 U.S. Open in Houston, Dave Marr recognized that the sands were running out. He figured that a "player like him" might qualify for ten or twelve U.S. Opens, and that half of those would be contested on courses where he felt good about his chances. He halved that number again for the times he might be playing well enough to contend. If you're scoring at home, that leaves three "legitimate" shots in a career, to say nothing of injury, unusual course conditions, bouts of food poisoning, thoughtless baggage handlers, camera phones, etc.

There are numerous other occupational hazards. Colin Montgomerie has written: "If you were to ask what irritates me most on the golf-course, it would not be the rustle of sweet paper, the crunching of crisps or someone moving in the crowd. To me, nothing is more maddening than the marshal with the 'Silence Please!' board who holds the notice aloft only at the last moment."

This is a good one readily on display at any tour event, and a rich vein of madness. Monty's acute sensitivities are well documented, as is the truly horrid treatment he's endured, particularly at the Brookline Ryder Cup. At his worst, though, he can bring out Fleet Street's raffish best. Long since inured to the tabloid press with their tidy headlines like "Monty Misery" and occasionally referred to as "Monty-ster," I wonder what he thought of this personal favorite. Mel Webb in *The Times* once described him as having "the mien of a bereaved yak." Yakish behavior notwithstanding; he was very pleasant to a group of us at Turnberry one afternoon. Things were actually quite chummy between Montgomerie and the gallery earlier that fateful week in Boston. There were smiles and banter. Everything was light and friendly—playful, not at all spiteful. That was before the home team dug its hole and then, of course, things turned ugly.

Why do marshals wait until the last moment to move? Perhaps their arms are tired. Whatever the reason, the scene has been played out countless times with perfect Marx Brothers-like pantomime. The player addresses his ball and is (finally!) ready to pull the trigger. A moment passes. Up shoots an arm from the marshal standing with his back to the golfer but squarely within his peripheral vision. Back steps the golfer, his train of thought effectively derailed. Down goes the marshal's arm. The routine starts anew. The player sniffs the air and starts fresh. And the insanity starts again.

Often as not the marshal is clueless that *he* is the distraction. That makes it even better, the straight man with his officious (maybe even a little Yak-like?) air. Blithely ignored by the galleries, ineffectual at his job, golf's rent-a-cop equivalent gets no respect. It can't help that he's dressed in an often ridiculous over-priced tournament shirt he's been forced to buy. It's not as if the Hell's Angels were guarding the stage at Altamont. Not to make light of a tragic and preventable death, but the pedestrian traffic tie-ups at a tour event, and the inherent difficulties presented by large mobile crowds can make for implacable situations, for players and spectators alike, without any additional attitude or mindlessness, least of all from those meant to maintain order. More is the pity. With ever longer courses, designed to be driven not walked, strategically roped off to prevent thousands of visitors from traveling as the crow flies, a unit of Army Rangers would find it a challenge to keep up with a feature pairing even moving at their typical snail's pace. Children and the elderly, of course, hardly stand a chance. At the Texas Open in San Antonio—a course admittedly not designed with spectators in mind—the golfers and caddies (with the occasional spouse, manager, child, etc. in tow) are shuttled by something called a golf cart from the 18th green to the 1st tee. This from the same folks who several years ago viewed Casey Martin, a courageous golfer with a brittle, withered leg, as some sort of subversive. For shame!

Those not important enough to commandeer a vehicle—and you truly do not rate at a tour event if you don't have a cart—were left to follow in vain by navigating a slippery slope of cedar chips and mud. Imagine! Pro golfers succumbing to the use of carts to get around a golf course. Given the tour's legal pomposity on the issue, talk about *chutzpah*. Could this same surreptitious phenomenon be taking place elsewhere on the PGA Tour?

Back on the tee, presumably it has been a long day for our volunteer marshal. The thrill of the experience has long since evaporated. At first excited to be around and readily acknowledged by the players as the days and shifts wear on, he becomes tired and discouraged; hardly anyone pays him any heed. He has been close to the action but has seen proportionately very little golf. In hindsight he should've taken the more coveted jobs in the press tent, driven a shuttle, or been stationed on one of the par threes; but, no, he's out here working in the heat with someone he doesn't know. It's hot and things aren't going particularly well. Perhaps his antics with the quiet sign, timed just right, are but a thinly disguised effort to exact a sliver of revenge. Monty, these guys know full well that they're tweaking you and the other sourpuss millionaires who look right through them and can't be bothered to sign their caps. This'll fix 'em, they figure. Or so I imagine.

At dawn, walking along the Old Course before the final round of the

Millenium Open, I chanced upon the entire assembled marshal crew. Dew was still heavy, steam rose from cups of coffee. Instead of the toucan-inspired shirts familiar to PGA Tour marshals back home, the men wore practical and stately Gore-Tex navy blue windbreakers. There was an undeniable martial air to the proceedings as they literally received their marching orders.

"You," they were told, "are the last line of defense between the players and the gallery." Indeed. Someday marshals could be forced to take on a much more serious role than merely milling about, a situation were it to take place that is difficult to comprehend, or prevent. During at least one post 9/11 PGA Tour stop, each pairing included not just the usual marker keeping scores, but also a casually-dressed member of the local police force. Their vulnerability must concern the players. The inherent openness of a golf course and their proximity to the fans is one of the pro game's pleasures. Someone could conceivably be carrying something more despicable than a cell phone. Little known, Tiger Woods regularly receives death threats, a reminder of the ever-present and unthinkable danger.

When the Open was last played in St. Andrews, London bombing attacks were still fresh in the mind. Michael Campbell, recently-crowned U.S. Open champion, expressed his anxiety. Despite a course that must present logistical nightmares to authorities, bordering not only the town but a beach, fortunately there were no incidents.

Back for a moment to Tiger's triumphant walk up the home fairway of the Millenium Open. The cover photo depicts the crush around the impending champion. Tiger is in his customary Sunday burgundy power color, along with his caddie, a mobile TV camera, the scoring markers, an announcer or two, several security types and, I believe it was, David Duval and his caddie. The crowd was soon pressed back forcibly by a line of marshals and police. I was lucky enough to have a unique vantage point to the fanfare. A small group of us were perched on a rooftop sipping very good champagne about halfway up the home fairway as evening encroached.

Golfers and entourage slowly made their way through the crowd. For some reason that year they were held back from their celebratory frolic behind the champion. Accounts in the next day's papers noted fans were pushed to the edge and even into the Swilcan Burn, an unpleasant prospect. The obligatory streaker sprang from the throng assembled around the historic home green. She was not unattractive, a topless dancer from Aberdeen who, we later learned, nearly cost her caddy husband his job. Her arrival was greeted by a chorus of ironic cheers. She gave Tiger a kiss, shuffled gaily over to the flag and twirled several times around it as if it were a Maypole before her illicit star turn came to an end.

Why the crowd was prevented from falling in behind Tiger per tradition was never explained. Perhaps there were legitimate security concerns, or merely worries of a stampede. Nothing about the change in protocol was mentioned at the early morning roll call. Understandably, people were, in the truest American sense of the term, pissed off about being denied their brush with glory.

Watching from such a terrific vantage point was a cherished highlight in a spotty career. I'm thankful to Gordon Begg, whose house it then was, and to Kyle Phillips, the course architect of the justifiably acclaimed Kingsbarns, who was kind enough to invite me along. What fun! What a moment!

Tiger's triumph was complete. There was one more special and completely unexpected—and unplugged—moment before we steadied ourselves for the descent down the outside spiral staircase to Gordon's kitchen. Tiger was receiving the Claret Jug diagonally across from us in front of the R & A. Behind him, down the fairway, past the crowds, now freed, St. Andreans were reclaiming their ancient parkland. People wandered and strolled oblivious to the formal ceremony. Gordon let out his old dog who gamboled off into the gloaming. In a corner of his kitchen sat a large cardboard box filled with golf balls. These were the sliced drives off the 18th tee that traveled about 170 yards and bounded down the staircase, and sometimes into the glass kitchen side door. In photos or paintings of the home hole, you'll notice a little white house set amongst the taller, grey stoned-hotels and clubs, about at Granny Clarke's Wynd for those familiar with the hole. That's the house.

Another photo doesn't quite do the scene justice. You'll have to take my word on it. Imagine a toddler on unsteady legs, his father rolling a stroller in pursuit. This was the scene that played out beneath us. The wee one clutched a cut-down club and was determinedly trying to strike his ball with steep axe-like blows amidst the crowd in the advancing twilight. It was priceless. Ahead, one illustrious player was being hailed the year's champion golfer and lifting the fabled trophy. Just beyond the limelight was, perhaps, another budding champion, his time to come. Oblivious to the commotion around him he was enthusiastically taking advantage of the Old Course as have his countrymen, old and young, for centuries. Of all the scenes I've been privileged to witness, this was the most memorable. Were it not for the photo, inexpert though it was, I'm not sure I would've believed it. But it happened and I won't soon forget it.

ten commandments
1. Play the first hole well.
2. Any golfer can use any type of swing that he can master.
3. Players who have holed out should not try their putts over again when other players are following them.
4. Don't panic until you get there. You might have a shot.
5. If you can't win in your dreams, forget it.
6. Length never made a golf course.
7. You think best when you are happiest.
8. Don't call anybody mister that you may have to play later on.
9. You are what you are, not what you do.
10. Aye, yon hole is four and quarter inches across, and the whole damned world is around it.

(1. Doug Ford. 2. Lee Trevino. 3. R&A, 1899. 4. Domingo Lopez. 5. Calvin Peete. 6. Bill Mehlhorn. 7. Peter Thomson. 8. Ben Hogan. 9. Harvey Penick. 10. Anonymous.)

"Good Lord, please let me get this airborne."

First tee prayer attributed to Betsy King reflecting on her first drive in a Solheim Cup.

three

•••• presidential pardon ••••

The years and golf's changing perceptions have done little to clarify the fine line that separates wholesome presidential recreation from dereliction of duty. Given the intense probing of even the most prosaic details (boxers or briefs?), it's hardly surprising that their golf somehow matters.

Those leaders pleading in H.L. Mencken's memorable phrase "guilty of golf" know their best efforts will be mediocre at best. They know that their golf—in other circumstances enjoyed within a private, nurturing environment—will likely be recorded, repeated, lampooned, scrutinized, discussed, analyzed and even vilified. If they're too good, they're not working enough. If they stink, well then. They also must live with knowing that their very presence on a course disrupts the golfing lives of a fierce, vocal constituency that needs their recreation as much as he does. Vice presidents can neither expect any immunity. The wake of destruction from Spiro Agnew's driver was shooting fish in a barrel for *Mad Magazine* and proficiency alone couldn't save the best golfer to come within a heartbeat of the Oval Office. Just the opposite. Dan Quayle's game was a launch pad to criticism, a running staple from *Doonesbury* to *Newsweek*. Its May 20, 1991 cover depicted the stylish Quayle follow-through alongside the headline: *The Quayle Handicap Is He a*

Lightweight—Or Smarter Than You Think? (Their verdict: inconclusive although his inexperience was deemed far more troubling than his golf, which was never mentioned in the articles.)

The golfing president must also contend with the inevitable entourage, his posse, including the guy carrying The Box, and the accumulated weight of the free world on his shoulders, troubling baggage to take to the first tee with a rusty gate. In the face of almost certain disaster, that these men continue to rely and even cling to golf—political fallout be damned—must say something about its significance and its allure.

A novel prescription, Woodrow Wilson was advised to take up the game on the recommendation of his personal physician. Despite his once having "yelled like a madman" at a Princeton baseball game (he apologized), by all accounts, the son of a Presbyterian minister and former Ivy League president, was a studious golfer.

Dr. Cary Grayson hoped golf would help ease Wilson's mind and calm his own fears of an impending presidential breakdown. The time would come as hopes for peace darkened, and Wilson weathered several personal tragedies including the death of his wife, that Grayson felt compelled to officially urge his patient to "slow up," and take some time out for golf, "or he could not keep going."

Either by coincidence or design, it is a matter of record that Wilson was on the golf course the day his nomination was secured, on the day the Lusitania was struck, and on the day war was formally declared on Germany; he having played, by his own admission, "almost every day" preceding the nation's entry into the 'War to End All Wars.'

Wilson holds an unusual presidential golf distinction: he played regularly with his wife, albeit his second wife. Franklin Roosevelt would later abandon an emotionally wrought Eleanor, a St. Andrews golf widow on their honeymoon. One FDR scholar believes golf typified the extent of their estrangement. Eleanor alleged that her husband rarely mentioned golf after the devastation of polio, but that is easily refuted.

Golf remained close to his heart; he just didn't talk about it with *her*, a scenario familiar to many addicts with a non-golfing spouse. Franklin liked to go down to Warm Springs and drive out to the course that he helped design to "shout bawdy advice to the players carrying with him a silver pitcher of martinis with which to toast good shots—and bad."

History notes that Wilson was still mourning the loss of his wife when he met the widow Galt with mud still on his boots from his constitutional round out at the Washington Golf Club in Arlington, traversing the route from which Wilson Boulevard takes its name. Their honeymoon suite at the Homestead overlooked the resort course.

"We played golf in the mornings, and took long motor trips in the afternoons," Edith Bolling Wilson wrote in her memoirs. She never forgot the impression made on their first chance meeting. The President was wearing what she took for a cheaply made "golfing suit." Dr. Grayson also wore duds from the same tailor. "They were," she dished, "*not* smart."

It wasn't concern for the commander-in-chief's sanity but a friend's feelings that later prompted Bobby Jones to council Dwight Eisenhower. A "congenital slicer," thanks in part to an old football injury-related knee surgery, Ike was not enjoying his game. Augusta National domo Clifford Roberts let slip that the president was being "badgered" into playing his own ball for 18 holes with discouraging results.

This "can produce mental and nervous pressures to which you should not be subjected on the golf course," cautioned Jones. He suggested a more relaxing—yet still competitive—four ball, best ball. Forget about double bogeys or worse. "I would just pick the darn thing up before that happens." Eisenhower wrote back, meekly, especially for a former Supreme Allied Commander, that he knew the advice was "at least academically sound. Whether I can put it into practice is another story." He promised to try.

In an October 1958 press conference, Eisenhower sought to explain the game's attraction. Along with fishing and hunting, golf provided mild outdoor exercise, just the thing needed for older folks. "And on top of it," he said, "it induces you to take at any one time two or three hours, if you can, where you are thinking of the bird or that ball or the wily trout. Now, to my mind it is a very healthful, beneficial kind of thing, and I do it whenever I get a chance, as you well know."

Before world war consumed his presidency, the nation and himself, Wilson seemed less concerned about any perceived negative political implications of his passion, at least for a time. In August 1916, he was asked by his re-election committee for a photo of him playing golf, "for political purposes." He was amenable with one hesitation written in longhand across the bottom of the page: "Ohhh—but not a movie. I play too badly!" Several months later, Europe engulfed in war and the U.S. entry inevitable, Wilson emphatically turned down a golf invitation. He wrote treasury secretary William McAdoo: "I would be a fool if I went into it. I don't care to have my golf exhibited just at this critical period of our country's history." Among his correspondence, in June of 1918, is a request from Chicago's Ridgemoor Golf Club. Could the president spare a couple of autographed golf balls, with his wife's signature included, for a Red Cross benefit? He could, the tip of a substantial golf iceberg of support benefiting the Allied cause, specifically the Red Cross.

Higher office has not precluded presidents from having to get their game in on the sly. When Gerald Ford could not stand it any longer, it was left to press secretary Ron Nessen to cover for the golfer who once quipped, "I know I'm getting better because I'm hitting fewer spectators." With all due respect, Mr. President, the joke, while humorous, doesn't stand up to scrutiny. Presumably galleries having been forewarned following well-publicized repeated bombardment began taking appropriate precautions. The tightly wrapped self-deprecating joke also carries the flavor of a professional courtesy extended by comedian Bob Hope; although Ford may have been onto something when he later joked that he'd helped the comedian, and regular golfing companion, "make a living off my game."

Nessen did his best. "I couldn't bring myself to look the press in the eye and say, "He wants to play golf and he's going to Florida to play golf," he confided years later. The White House press corps was advised that the official rationale for the trip was a "community meeting."

Joe Murdoch, co-founder of the Golf Collectors Society, produced an undated newspaper clipping regarding what may stand as the first passing presidential acquaintance with golf. The clip alludes to Ulysses S. Grant's sojourns abroad after leaving office. Grant extensively toured Scotland, spending twenty days there in September 1877. The guest of various dukes, he visited numerous areas where golf was popular, including Dornoch, Edinburgh, Ayr, and his ancestral home of Grant town. He was awarded the freedom of the city of Glasgow and Edinburgh, and generally enjoyed himself. According to author John Russell Young, "though the weather was unfavorable, the General took deep interest in studying the agricultural system of the North of Scotland." Grant does not specifically refer to golf but he could conceivably have witnessed the game. The clipping mentions a demonstration that included several whiffs. Apocryphal as it sounds, Grant responded that the game seemed like good exercise but he failed to see the purpose of the ball. Ho!Ho! (This also sounds surprisingly like he might have been working behind the scenes with one of Hope's legendary writers, but this too is unverified.)

We do know that when the Library of Congress was established in 1800, the extensive private collection of nearly 6,500 volumes belonging to Thomas Jefferson did not include a single golf book. Perhaps it's no surprise that the Sage of Monticello's encyclopedic interests did not include golf. He sensibly once wrote: "Of all exercises, walking is best."

The Bush family's distinguished lineage with the United States Golf Association notwithstanding (two past presidents), the game has never had a more staunch golf advocate in The White House than William Howard Taft.

Taft's unyielding advocacy should not be underestimated. The game clearly appealed to his judicial mien and, echoing Eisenhower's comments, his quest for gentle exercise. "Golf in the interest of good health and good manners," he once said. "It promotes self-restraint and affords a chance to play the man and act the gentleman." Candidly unathletic, to the delight of cartoonists, the 300-pounder who never desired the office, once found himself stuck in the White House bath tub. Golf was "his chief vacation diversion," he said, often pursued at a delightful and recommended relic, Murray Bay in rural Quebec. Unlike his coy successors, the judge was not shy about revealing his scores (the other side of 100) nor was he averse to audibly conversing with his ball. "Pshaw!" and his self-deprecating characterization of his game as "bumble-puppy" were frequent comments. (Bumble-puppy?)

Big Bill stuck to his guns about golf against not only his political mentor, but the most dominant figure of his era. Theodore Roosevelt was many things, as Red Smith would later say about Branch Rickey, he was a man "of many facets, all of them turned on." The one thing that TR was not was a golfer. In addition to his more manly outdoor pursuits, he played tennis like a crazy man, gripping the racket halfway up the handle. He served the ball by hitting it out of his left hand without a toss. He was also very, very careful, as he advised his chosen successor, to avoid any photos of him doing so. "It seems absurd," he wrote in a letter that he specified not be seen by anyone other than Taft or his wife, "but I am convinced that the prominence that has been given to your golf playing has not been wise, and from now on I hope your people will do everything they can to prevent one word being sent out about either your fishing or your playing golf." He hoped Taft would exercise self-restraint, viewing the game as politically "fatal."

Taft ignored him, defying Roosevelt's repeated entreaties to keep quiet about it, particularly on the campaign stump. "With only a few moments of self-exaltation," he told a California audience "...we Americans, who are not celebrated for our modesty, may find such a game excellent training."

Of course, Teddy Roosevelt presented a vigorous physical contrast to his portly successor; Taft remained a man of conviction. Twas true, building a tee out of sand was a bother for him; as one chronicler kindly noted, "Stooping...is not his favorite sport." Still, there were caddies to do that. One report notes he commendably played 18 holes at the Myopia Hunt Club in Massachusetts in under two hours. "That means good going," wrote a reporter with deferential, if inexpert enthusiasm. "In short, he is a very good golfer indeed." Taft struggled to break 100, never took a lesson in his life ("save for the school of experience"), and employed an unconventional baseball swing. "The President is a good example of the ball player who, having taken to golf, plays his golf in a baseball way," James Drew told readers of *The Independent*. He ended his profile on a high note: "He rarely misses a ball."

Roosevelt may have been vexed but Taft, the first president to throw out the first ball at a baseball game (much more politically palatable), swept the electoral college vote, and narrowly won the popular vote; this despite the "literally hundreds of letters" in protest to his golf that Roosevelt alleged receiving (none of which, incidentally, survive). As was true throughout the twentieth century, the presidential bounce to golf popularity was undeniable. Frances Ouimet would win the 1913 U.S. Open, a historic triumph to be sure, but a president's stamp of approval was something else entirely. Taft's outspoken support for the game's democratic leanings lent it credibility. *The New York Times* reported that the president was responsible for a "great increase in the number of players this year (1909)" at Van Cortlandt Park in the Bronx, and elsewhere. "Last year it used to be tennis," said "keeper" Tom

White, "because that was President Roosevelt's hobby. Now the tennis courts are almost deserted, except for the habitual players."

That Taft's great-grandson's golf may have crossed the moral and ethical tenets so revered by his ancestor would undoubtedly have aggrieved the bumble puppy golfer. Ohio Governor Robert Taft's four counts of ethics violations in 2005 relating to the venerable family penchant for the game await their legal finding. One assumes that despite the perennial allegations of politicians behaving badly with golf, the game is innocent. Any chicanery between politicians and golf invariably speaks more directly to the former than to the latter.

There is a dreary sameness to these allegations. Insider access to government contractors. Illicit campaign contributions. Public servants behaving like private servants. Only the names and the destinations change, as exemplified by this telling excerpt (Not!) from an Oval Office press conference held by Gerald Ford on September 30, 1976.

> **Q.** Mr. President, in your golf outings, or social occasions, or other vacations with Rod Markley of Ford Motor Company or U.S. Steel, did you discuss government business with them either when you were a Member of the House, or Vice President, or President?
>
> **Ford.** Not to my best recollection.
>
> **Q.** You never discussed business?
>
> **Ford.** No.

Next question. Numerous junkets have been built around the perception that golf has served captains of industry as a useful, even necessary, capitalist tool. Skeptical, several years ago I put the question to then-Shell Oil President, Chairman and CEO Steven Miller. He was insistent that golf was an asset. "Absolutely, the golf course or sitting around just before or after has probably been my most frequent place where I have done deals." Never having been a captain, let alone an ensign, of industry, I remain unconvinced. Further testimony comes from former Andersen Consulting CEO George Shaheen. With respect to doing deals on the golf course, he told *Golf & Meetings Magazine (August 2001):*

"No, that's balderdash. [Who knew captains of industry still used words like balderdash?!] Again, you use golf to get to know people. Not just their golf ability but things like their adherence to tradition, to the rules of the game, how they conduct themselves, how they're dressed, and how they treat others, be it a caddie or someone else. It's a game where you can take the true measure of a person."

Depending upon one's view of the man and the office, Warren Gamaliel Harding stands as either dishonest, incompetent, in over his head, and a philanderer, perpetually ranked as one of the worst presidents in the Republic's history, OR, variations of the above and a not atypical example of the American 20th century adult male. As it happens, there can be no doubt that he was a "real" golfer.

The scandals that engulfed his term, and his political fortunes aside, Harding's commitment to sports and specifically to golf are unimpeachable. "For Harding," according to historian Francis Russell, "the sports page was the most interesting section of the paper." The same has certainly been true for many of his successors, not to mention, of course, countless Americans.

Harding's golf would land him on a less flattering section of the paper, the front page. He told Grantland Rice that he "made a point" of playing at least three afternoons a week while in office, a frequency that would rank favorably with any aside from Wilson before a disabling stroke. Harding, who served on the USGA governing board and briefly as a committeeman, had his informal golfing "cabinet," a vestige of his days in the U.S. Senate. That wasn't what got him in hot water. Nor was it the regular poker cabinet convened twice a week nightly in the White House. His most serious breach was an ancient one, caught playing golf on the Sabbath. He quickly recanted. His press secretary was called in for damage control. *The New York Times* reprinted George Christiansen's terse denial as front page news: "The President does not play Sunday golf and he has no intention of doing so." Back in the day this was no small offense. Were Harding caught on the Old Course during the time of divine service in 1599, after several increasing fines, a third offense would find him placed on the "repentance pillar." The fourth offense meant being "deprived of office." Don't like the sound of the repentance pillar. Indeed, the Scottish variation on the Dutch "jougs" or "shame pole" would typically imprison the penitent in an iron collar, perhaps lead lined and attached by a short chain to a post, pillar or wall. The offender would thus be exposed to the torment of fellow citizens (rocks, mud, excrement, etc.) similar to the harassment commonly inflicted on those interred in the stocks. An appealing remedy for today's political malfeasance, perhaps, if inhumane.

A proponent of Prohibition, Harding nevertheless liked to drink, liberally if not heavily. To the chagrin of school teachers and anti-smoking advocates, it was also well known that he smoked and worse. At least one notable constituent was nonplussed. "Harding is all right," said Thomas Edison. "Any man who chews tobacco is all right." With the coming of spring, Harding beat balls out on the south lawn. His efforts in training his Airedale Laddie Boy to retrieve them, however, proved unsuccessful. He preferred six dollar Nassaus and was not averse to presses or side bets; a Secret Service man was enlisted to keep the books. A ball in a bunker cost a dollar; pars paid off big, $5. Accounts of his golf are suspiciously complimentary. There are repeated claims of his knack for pulling off passable short lofted lob shots when needed. As opposed to Richard Nixon, once caught by Sam Snead employing the *hand mashie* when it appeared a bazooka could not free him from trouble, or Bill Clinton, who was taken to task for a liberal view of the mulligan and the 14-club rule,

Harding braved the rub of the green. When advised a ribbed niblick he was using was non-conforming, he pulled it right out of his bag. "Take it and give to some caddie," H.B. Martin reported him saying. Harding was not looking for nor expected executive privilege especially with gimmes, a trait he shared with Ronald Reagan who, if Tom Watson is to be believed, refused to accept anything outside the leather. Harding carried an old Spanish Armada coin that he used to determine the order of play on the first tee; he would not freely assume the honor. "Forget that I am President of the United States," he would say. "I'm Warren Harding, playing with some friends, and I'm going to beat hell out of them." During the transition he won praise of a sort from a reliable source, the recipient—from Harding—of the 1921 U.S. Open trophy. "He certainly is a regular fellow," said "Long" Jim Barnes, as diplomatic an appraisal of one's golf if ever there was one.

Patience was considered one of Harding's golfing virtues. "He has been known to throw a club ahead of him in disgust," former Oregon senator Jonathan Bourne shared with the *American Golfer*, "but never to break one on the ground in rage." Undeterred by rain or thunderstorms, as, incidentally, was Taft, he was better at match than medal play, and preferred "the struggle of close contest...than he does in having a walkover and beating by seven or eight up." He believed that he closed well—playing stronger as the round progressed. Harding, and Eisenhower, who left a trail of golf spikes through the Oval Office carpet, have been described by historians as "golf compulsives." (There are worse vices.) Harding could have given either of his predecessors two a side. Instead, he gave Taft the only job Big Bill truly coveted, an appointment to become Chief Justice of the Supreme Court. Presidents come and go, Taft said, but the court goes on forever.

By the early twenties golf was still a cause for electoral concern.

Typical complaints centered on the game's association with privilege and elitism, the sport of Rockefeller, Carnegie and Schwab. Interestingly, less was made of Harding, Taft or Wilson taking time away from the office, a more frequently cited modern charge. (Perhaps Teddy Roosevelt's enjoinders against ever being photographed in tennis "costume" were well-founded. Footage of George H.W. Bush happily playing golf in Kennebunkport juxtaposed with televised images of the first Gulf War served as an arresting, and potentially politically damaging, contrast.)

His first day as the official Republican nominee, Harding suffered a phalanx of reporters and cameras on the golf course. The commotion ruined his first drive. Enough was made of his swing ("youthful…and makes many a sweet spot") that when he started showing up in newsreels, campaign advisors circled. One sympathetic senator noted that sequences of Harding, dressed in his customary plus fours with tassels, were met with stony silence in one movie theater. "I don't believe the golf business arouses any enthusiasm," he cautioned. Again came reports of hundreds of letters criticizing his participation in a "rich man's game, a mollycoddle game." There followed a confidential exchange: "Show this to the Senator. *I want him to see It.*" As he would later with his Sunday golf, Harding got the message. He stopped performing in front of the cameras until after the election. With motor vehicle registrations mushrooming to over nine million from barely 400,000 a decade before, motoring was deemed a more publicly palatable avocation. A fawning account of his pre-presidential life, published soon after the election, almost apologetically acknowledges golf.

"Golf and *autoing* are favorite pastimes of the President," wrote Sherman Cuneo in *From Printer to President*, " though the former is a recreation of very recent times, and only since 1915, when he became a temporary resident of Washington." It's as if golf were just another of those repugnant, inevitable and unavoidable vices of life in a corrupt capital.

The transition left ample time on the fine and now sadly bulldozed under Donald Ross course at the Ponce de Leon resort in St. Augustine,

Florida where Harding retreated to select a cabinet and decompress. Golf references became more frequent, got more play and were deferentially upbeat. *The Literary Digest* picked up J.L. Wright's account of his game ("I have seen him drive 275 yards. He is also a very strong putter...") from *The American Golfer*, shortly after the election. Just before the inauguration, a New Yorker wintering in Palm Beach, found much to like in his game. H.K. Wilcox of Middleton, a "club champ in Orange County," thought the President's game exhibited traits that boded well for the nation. He told a *New York Times* reporter: "Mr. Harding plays a good game, drives straight, carries through and keeps his eye on the ball, a good omen, I think, for the next four years." Clearly a corner had been turned with golf. An additional boost would come in the decade that would herald the giants of sport's golden age with Bobby Jones front and center.

Newly installed in the White House, in the Spring of 1921, Harding invited sportswriters Grantland Rice and Ring Lardner to join him for a round. Rice was complimentary about his host's "good average game." He later sent some clubs which Harding gratefully acknowledged. The President did however have an unfortunate habit. Before others had played he would obliviously leave the teeing ground. He nearly paid the price, placing himself dangerously in the line of fire as Lardner was about to slice his drive. It bore low and close enough to the President, standing some 40 yards up the fairway, to sever a branch which fell on him. "I did all I could to make (vice president) Coolidge president," Lardner told Harding. The quip elicited a robust presidential laugh.

To this convivial scene—not on this exact day but in Harding's golf orbit—imagine the addition of a young caddie. The boy had been raised in rural Maine, one of ten children in an orthodox Jewish family. A decent athlete, he caddied with his friends during the Maine summers, often drawing a bag from one of the numerous vacationing millionaires escaping the heat in Bar Harbor. One day he caddied for a congenial golfer, a big man who hit a big but occasionally erratic ball, and Shirley, for that was the boy's unusual name, excelled himself in the pursuit and retrieval of lost golf balls. The amiable golfer was much impressed by the lad. He tipped him two dollars when seventy-five cents was typical, and a dime not unfamiliar. Two dollars was unheard of.

Thus began a remarkable, fantastically improbable story, one of those made only-in-America, or as Shirley Povich recalled in a cherished letter, a "fairy-tale story."

Povich's patron was none other than Edward B. McLean, the owner of the *Washington Post*. He took a shine to the boy, and sent his Rolls around to pick him up whenever he played. At the end of the summer he invited the new high school grad to come to Washington, attend college at his expense, and take a job at the paper. That he did. Arriving in Washington, Shirley again set about caddieing for McLean. This time it was at his own private course, at Friendship, McLean's private estate on Wisconsin Avenue. The eccentric, and often extravagant publisher had taken to golf in a big way. He was eager to improve sufficiently to beat his good friend, the president, and went so far as to hire U.S. Open champion Leo Diegel as a private tutor, and he had Diegel follow him up to Maine. The games at Friendship were joyous affairs and often included other early pros like Bobby Cruickshank, Freddie McLeod or the first Texas Open champion, Bob McDonald. The surreal scene at the surreal oasis—18 holes with one double green, included waiters standing by with trays of illicit "refreshment." All this Povich conveyed several years before his death. One day, instead of grabbing McLean's bag, Shirley was introduced to a guest. "Mr. President, this is Shirley Povich. He's the best caddie in the United States and he's going to caddie for you today." Shirley had no idea what McLean was talking about. Then he recognized Harding standing there in the flesh, Secret Service agents hovering nearby. H.B. Martin wrote in *Fifty Years of American Golf* that Harding "frequently...scored in the low eighties." His discerning caddie remembered it differently. The first president born after the Civil War, and the first after WWI, was a "lousy golfer," he wrote, who "tried to flirt with 100. But no question of his passion for the game. On many an occasion he played the West Potomac Park public course just south of the White House."

Straight out of high school, enrolled to study law at Georgetown, as invited, Shirley had raced down to the paper and was given a job on the city desk as a copy boy. Two years later he was covering sports. His last column for the *Post*, the last of an estimated 17,000 culled for an anthology, ran seventy-five years later, on June 5th, 1998. He passed away the following day. "What a life," he closed his letter. "What a world then. What wealth (no income tax). What gladness that I was a little piece of it." What other game could deliver such a magical storyline?

four

•••••hello bob•••••

Woodrow Wilson once referred in a speech to the "quick comradeship of letters." It was a "very real comradeship," he said, "because it is a comradeship of thought and of principle." Delivery methods may more quickly speed our thoughts and principles across the globe, but the personal letter has no more endearing competition. We turn, then, to another fleeting and unplugged example of quick camaraderie, shared in this case between two dear friends and, once, fierce competitors.

His playing days behind him, Bob Jones in his late fifties and into his early sixties still entertained a near endless stream of requests from a loyal public. Correspondence from the genteel to the shamelessly atavistic were treated with equanimity. Against the backdrop of his deteriorating health, keeping up must've been both welcome and tiresome, flattering and fatiguing. An enormous USGA bequest reveals an admirable, almost obligatory sense of duty. What Herbert Warren Wind described as his "generosity of spirit" is undeniable in perusing binder after binder of letters revealing Jones being Jones.

Fan letters were rarely as well thought out as their inevitably timely, and occasionally, wry response. Admirers sought photos, autographs, product endorsements, remembrances and confirmation of past brushes with glory, and his opinions. They sent articles, clippings and comic strips recalling his exploits. They offered crack cures and a raft of invitations, from the University of St. Andrews to Georgia Tech, from Republican fundraisers to bowling alley openings. ("Bobby, you have contributed so much to the advancement of sports," reads one appeal, "that we also want you to be a part of the opening of our new bowling center.") Broadview Bowl-O-Matic received his every wish for success; his health providing a convenient excuse for declining all but the most obligatory commitments.

Others sought his investment or the Jones name in legitimizing golf practice aids. One appeal was accompanied by schematics as if plucked from a Heath Robinson cartoon. These mixed with the routine flow of active business, family, and informal correspondence from friends, associates, doctors, well wishers, and acquaintances going back decades.

An Atlantan expressing the urge "to do something extra for our fellow man and for our good old State of Georgia," proposed sharing his personal "Neuro-Therapy" discoveries. When might he drop by to "talk shop?" Perhaps suppressing a more earthy reply, Jones comes as close to exasperation as a Southern gentleman battling a crippling spinal disease would publicly allow himself. Two days after Christmas, 1959, he perused the cheery promises: "No Drugs and no Medicine …and I have proven it on myself …and on some of my friends who were not too well. Now they too are thrilled. …If I was a betting man I would bet that it could mean an extra 20 to 25 years added to my life." Jones wrote back:

> I hope you will know that I cannot be anything but deeply grateful to you for your interest. I also hope you will understand when I tell you that having wasted about ten years trying to find something to improve my physical condition, I some time ago concluded that I did not have any more time to throw away. I think I need all my

117
•

time and energy to devote to activities more likely to
have some success. With all good wishes and many
thanks, Most sincerely, Robert T. Jones, Jr.

In his letters, Jones refers to his health only in passing. Often, like the
weather it is just another topic of conversation. Several letters regarding
his condition nevertheless stand out among the more mundane material
in the collection. His deterioration is evident in an exchange of notes
with the chief occupational therapist at the Georgia Warm Springs
Foundation (September 1958). Muriel F. Driver requests another interview to tweak the fork holder that a foundation bracemaker has been
working on specifically for Jones. (He responds the next day that he's
been trying to reach her to make an appointment.)

"I think I asked you all sorts of questions, but I still have one that I
did not think of before," he queried neurosurgery pioneer Dr. Gilbert
Horrax at Boston's Lahey Clinic, in early March 1951, having given the
go-ahead for "another crack at my spine."

"Supposing that you were unable to remove the disc and are only
able to open the dura," he asks, "may I expect any relief from the pain I
now have in my back and left shoulder and the disability and discomfort
in my hands and arms?" That's about as explicit as the admissions get.
Horrax's reply, relayed to Jones's doctors in Atlanta, was not encouraging: "A stellate sympathetic block might be performed and I should be
glad to do this but I have no feeling that it would relieve the pain."

When he famously journeyed to St. Andrews for the last time in
1958 to become a Freeman of the Royal Burgh, several polite inquiries
on the same subject awaited him upon his return to Atlanta. All wanted
to know where did he get the golf car, the "electric trolley" Henry
Longhurst was shown driving him around the Old Course in a photo
that ran in *The Times*, both men bundled in topcoats. His referrals to the
good folks at Sears, Roebuck are enough that the reader starts to wonder
if Jones shouldn't have been on commission. His replies were invariably

decorously formal, if cordial. Formal but never form letters. Bob Jones didn't send form letters.

His final visit to St. Andrews struck a deep chord setting off a flurry of warm feelings back and forth across the Atlantic. The elegiac overtones could not dampen his spirits, nor the spirit of the occasion. To the Scots he was still Bobby. The emotional outpouring in print is quite moving. The remaining letters verify that the sincerity of the moment was not embellished or hyped by the subsequent army of chroniclers.

One St. Andrean wrote him, "You may be stricken now Bobby but you have the supreme consolation that you achieved "greatness"—also the comfort that you are well loved." Henry Cotton sent his regards from London. ("Anyway, this is to say Hello! from a boyhood admirer, who aspired to be a second Bobby Jones—but missed.") A small Scottish club sent a welcoming telegram. Jones had keenly hoped to hook up with old friends, British amateur greats Cyril Tolley and Roger Wethered, but it fell through to his lasting regret. Someone else wrote to sell him a rug depicting the Old Course.

Accorded the full privileges of a burgess and a guild brother, the golfer who impetuously tore up his card on his first turn on the Old Course was now, said Provost Robert Leonard at the historic ceremony: "one of our own number, officially now, as he has been so long unofficially." The privileges allowed Jones to dry his washing upon the opening and home fairways, though there is no evidence of his ever having done so.

Jones took particular delight in letters from children. His responses are devoid of even the hint of adult condescension or saccharine patronage. They wrote to tell him about their good shots, about getting their first sets of clubs, and to ask for his advice. "I'm not supposed to play softball or skate but I can play golf and mommie says you are a champ in golf and a better champ at living. I hope I can be kinda like you," one wrote "Mr. Bob" in 1958. The great amateur's reply asked that mommie be told he would "always treasure…your fine letter."

Hotel MIRAMAR
MOHAMMEDIA (MAROC)

Tél.: 20-21/2/3 · Télex : 21.964 "MIROTEL-MHDIA" Maroc Thursday, May 5 '66

Hello Bob

Hear we are ready to leave for Rome, Finished hear yesterday with Tom Weiskof and Roberto De Vicenso, Roberto playd beautful golf, But Tom not to good, Has a lot to learn,

The course was very dry, They dont have any water in System here, and rain is very scarse, The natives play very little golf, mostly tourist, But not many American, Germans, French, Visitors from northern Europe, where its still Winter, This does not have to much to offer for the Yankee,

Our Gallery was mostly navy personel from near by Base, In order to give it Native atmosphere They had to hire forty Camel riders, They smelld like a Goats,

The trip over was very nice But the time was to long for the Squire, seven hours to Paris with out sleep, Two hours hold over and three hours down

Route 4, Crest
Clinton, Tenn
April 18, 1965

Dear Mr. Jones,

I am a boy of 11 years of age and play golf. I have a 97 stroke average and like to play very much.

I have read your book, Golf is My Game and find it interesting. I have designed a course and wish you would tell me what you think about it.

Please answer my letter and tell me faults you find, and if it is okay do you think it will sell and for how much.

Thank you,
Chip Kendrick

April 22, 1965

Mr. Chip Kendrick
Route 4
Crest Drive
Clinton, Tennessee

Dear Chip:

I have looked over your plan. I am happy that
you are interested in golf and I admire your enterprise.

I think I should tell you that I do think that
your arrangement is a little bit out of proportion
because, for example, your parking lot appears to
occupy almost as much space as your golf course.

Why not ask your father to get for you a book on
golf course architecture? Or perhaps you might find
one at your public library.

Incidentally, you may have me confused with the
Robert Trent Jones who is a golf course architect,
which I am not. His address is 20 Vesey Street,
New York Ciry, in case you care to write him.

Most sincerely,

Robert T. Jones, Jr.

RTJ:jsm
Encls.

"Dear Mr. Jones, I am a boy of 11 years of age and play golf," begins another. "I have a 97 stroke average and like to play very much."

Resigned to routinely waiting six-to-eight weeks after sending in his box tops for redemption, imagine the delight when within a couple of days after 11-year old Chip Kendrick wrote to ask Jones for some tips on course design, he had his reply.

In his April 1965 letter, Jones assured him he had "looked over" the plan. There is no reason to think otherwise. "I am happy you are interested in golf and I admire your enterprise," he wrote. He does express concern that the area set aside for the parking lot appears on the drawing larger than the golf course itself. Perhaps, he suggests, a visit to the library is in order. Although the boy mentions having read *Golf is my Game*, Jones wonders if he still might have been confused with the course architect of the same name. He takes the liberty of including Trent Jones's Manhattan office address, just in case. This may not seem like much, but it is a pleasant image for the mind's eye: the champion in declining health scrutinizing a child's drawing as he plows through the imposing stack of morning mail, dictating replies to secretary Jean Marshall. In these days of computer-generated responses with stamped superstar signatures, such consideration on behalf of a young stranger is heartening. It is conjecture to speculate that these letters provided Jones with a respite from his physical pain, but a writer's pleasure in communicating his thoughts and principles to a shrinking but still appreciative world surely should not be discounted.

Jones naturally abhorred being taken advantage, and the New York City Better Business Bureau weathered the sort of channeled invective that can only come from someone frustrated by poor health with an active legal mind and ample time and resources, who has not yet received his $4.95 pocket telescope.

Ordered through "the shopping guide of some national magazine," Jones's cancelled check arrived but, months later, still no telescope. His one-man campaign switched into high gear. "The issue, as far as I am concerned," he wrote the BBB on July 2, 1958, one of several letters through spring and early summer, "now vastly transcends my interest in the telescope." Finally, three weeks later, after additional jabs, the promised pocket telescope arrived and the matter was resolved.

When the following year his new deluxe color television showed signs of chronic misbehavior, a team of experts scrambled, including the president of RCA Frank Folsom, the head of the RCA Service Company, and representatives from Atlanta's local NBC affiliate station. "At this point," Jones wrote Folsom in mock despair, "I wish to heaven I had back my remote control RCA black and white, but they say it is darkest before dawn. We will keep at it." Channel 2 was apparently having an unrelated problem with their color reception that complicated matters, but to the undoubted relief of Charles M. Odorizzi, Group Executive VP Consumer Products and Services—who also got an officious thank you note from Jones—and unspecified numbers of repairmen, the planets eventually aligned and the barmy set performed as advertised.

Christmas meant lots of deliveries and another opportunity to catch up with old friends. In 1959, Coca-Cola titan Bob Woodruff sent handkerchiefs ("perfectly beautiful and vitally useful," replied Jones). There were apples from Gene Sarazen, spiced beef from Nashville sportswriter Fred Russell. Bob Hope sent salt and peppers. A problem with a pair of overly narrow Christmas slippers from his daughter created a typical Jones paper trail that led up and down the chain of command at FR Tripler and Co. in New York. The "Outfitters to Gentlemen" didn't have half sizes, unfortunately, but they offered to have a pair specially made in England; they'd also run out of the blue and the red in size 10. The earnest replies and equally earnest follow-ups traveled back and forth between Atlanta and New York with the velocity of a daytime drama. Finally, a breakthrough: "We have sent a pair in brown. We do hope that you will find them most satisfactory." He did.

Ever the sportsman, Jones remained an avid fan and was not averse to chiming in when he couldn't help himself. Georgia Tech's heartbreaking loss to Auburn, 7 to 6 in late October 1959, was one such occasion. The mishap triggered wistful memories of a difficult lesson from his days as a competitor.

"I know from some very difficult experiences that the most dangerous thing in golf is to adopt a defensive attitude in order to protect even a moderate lead," he gently counseled Tech coach Bobby Dodd. He then launches into a detailed descant on behalf of keeping the ball rather than kicking it away. Jones closed with a disclaimer: "Obviously, I am writing about a game I know practically nothing about. What caused it all was a wondering if your boys, or any boys, can play as well trying to protect something as they can going all-out aggressive to win the game. Do not bother to answer this. We will talk about it next time we meet. Meantime, best of luck for the rest of the season and regards." In another aside, Jones remembers the notorious 1916 game in which the Yellow Jackets trounced Cumberland College of Tennessee 222 to 0. "Tech had a fine team that year," he recalled, "but Cumberland was not even a good high school. They had to scout around for enough players to field a team, and I believe had some players on the squad who had never played in a college game before." Grantland Rice also saw that game. He wrote that Cumberland's "greatest individual play…was when fullback [G.E. George] Allen circled right for a six-yard loss."

Of course, when it came to golf, Jones' intellectual quiver remained full. His letters reveal a running, incisive commentary. He pulled few punches. A fan happened on a Jim Murray column from the *Oakland Tribune*, circa April 1965, and mailed it to Jones. "Interested in knowing what you think re: this article" was scrawled across the top. What did *he* think?

The previous week Jack Nicklaus had won his second green jacket at the Masters, trouncing his nearest rivals Arnold Palmer and Gary Player by nine strokes. Jones had been particularly effusive in praising Jack's victory. Murray, however, was looking farther afield for something to write about. He was "as thrilled with Old Nick's victory as the next guy," but what about the liberally drawn field? What about the past champions and amateurs with no hope of contending? The cherished Masters invitation process (a tradition cherished particularly by Jones), has been at times as arcane as papal selection and long a sensitive subject. It would soon surface in stark color contrasts as professional golf confronted its own deep-seated racism. But that was not Murray's beef—not this time, anyway.

"...as they say around the race track," Murray pondered, "who did he [Nicklaus] beat? I'll tell you who: Chen Ching Po, Jack McGowan, Tomo Ishii, Richard Davies, Kel Nagel and Dean Beman, to name a few. He also beat Dr. Ed Upedgraff, Herman Keiser, Henry Picard, Gene Sarazen, if you want to know. Also John Hopkins, the amateur, not the hospital."

This, he posited, was golf's finest hour?

> I think I detect one wee fault with the Masters I hadn't thought about before. It's like a top-hole Broadway show. I mean, the proscenium arch is breathtaking, the book and lyrics all-time, the leading players the theater's best. But the supporting cast was shipped in from a road company of the "Hot Mikado."

Jones was not amused. This would not be the last, albeit here indirect exchange of a difference of opinion between Mr. Jones and Mr. Murray. The two would clash over Jones's reluctance to extend Charlie Sifford a Masters invitation, an obvious discriminatory omission no matter how expertly couched the denials.

"...Mr. Murray has every right to express any opinion he may hold," Jones wrote the fan. "For our part, we feel that ample opportunity to qualify for our tournament has been provided to all players whose absence Mr. Murray laments."

He wasn't through. Jones then imparts a crystalline insight on golf's major championships. "In all my forty years of experience in tournament golf, I have found that the more important tournaments are customarily won by a mere handful of players. It has always been the case that many players who shine brilliantly in minor tournaments fade rather dismally when the top prize becomes of major importance." You can almost hear the gavel drop. Case dismissed. Be gone.

In an amusing rant, Herb Graffis, then the publisher of *Golfdom, The Magazine of Golf Business*, wrote to Jones in May 1965, regarding the PGA of America's annual meeting. Today, the association bestows the Herb Graffis Cup in honor of one of the organization's "most noted contributors." He would no doubt have found it amusing that the organization now annually holds its fall trade show in Las Vegas. Then also the co-founder of the National Golf Foundation, Graffis couldn't believe what he was seeing:

> Here is golf, a pro game that never has had any sniff or stain of professional gambling, associating itself with the one place in the United States that a federal grand jury studies because of its management by organized criminals. Las Vegas is the only place low enough to welcome the Clay-Patterson fight. Las Vegas uses pro golfers as shills for crap games and peddles pros as an attraction like the naked, shapely and delicately scented show broads (go after 'em, Granpa, give Satan and them other sons of bitches cuts on their asses with you all's sword of fire.) I just can't get myself reconciled to going along with the idea of Las Vegas running golf, and it sure is doing it in demanding and getting the dates it wants on the PGA Schedule.

"Dear Herb," Jones responded, obviously tickled, "Your most recent letter is a classic. It has given me enjoyment and merriment. I am, of course, taking it home for [wife] Mary to read and making a copy to send to Cliff [Roberts]."

Courtesy Jack Nicklaus Museum

This most interesting piece of Nicklaus ephemera shows the young Jack was diligent about his golf while letting his mother know his whereabouts.

With old friends like Graffis, Gene Sarazen, or sportswriter Al Laney, long an admirer who understood the game, Jones felt free to confide and relax. He could speak his mind to confreres, like himself, as he once presumed of Laney, "too old fashioned to be in step with the new generation."

Change could be sometimes hard to fathom. Color televisions could go on the blink, the stymie could go the way of wood shafts, but he did like that Nicklaus boy. "Incidentally," he wrote Laney, after the 1965 PGA Championship (Jack finished tied for second), "did you ever see anything like the play of Jack Nicklaus around the greens at Laurel Valley? We have all been so overwhelmed by the power of this lad that we have almost overlooked his artistry in the short game. The chip he holed on the 71st hole from against the fringe and the immensely delicate shot he played from behind the 18th green were nothing short of miraculous. Please forgive my extravagances."

Laney was then still writing for the *New York Herald Tribune*. He first laid eyes on Nicklaus as a schoolboy phenom at the 1955 U.S. Amateur.

He would need convincing about the prodigy, which came in time; he later wrote of the immensity of Jack's game, but he agreed here with Jones. The kid's artistry around the greens rekindled thoughts of Walter Hagen, no small praise from someone who could take a long view. "It pleased me enormously that you spoke of Nicklaus's short game," he wrote back. "How many have observed that this was the one thing that might keep him from being a truly great one but that it improves? He has worked and it showed at Laurel Valley. Yes Indeed. I think he was a bit out of his mind at Bellerive, having talked about power so much but he is a most intelligent young man and was bound to see things the right way."

Jones took a genuine interest in the rising star. Too much should not be made of this, but their relationship, or "friendship" (as Jack would refer to it), represents a unique and noteworthy cross generational camaraderie. Unquestionably, whenever it blooms, a personal connection with the past has been quote-unquote good for the game. Nicklaus would write of the Jones tie that it made him "feel a part of an immensely worthwhile tradition." When an older player, a Henry Picard helps a Ben Hogan, or a Byron Nelson helps a Tom Watson, a bridge of respect transcends time. These connections distinguish golf from the other professional sports who honor their past heroes from across a chasm separated by money, speed, size and time; the ancients having little in common with the current generation of stars. Progress will always intrude, even in golf. The game changes: Jones could only marvel over Jack's prowess, "unfamiliar" he said as it was from his own game. Long ago, Old Tom Morris and predecessor Allen Robertson parted over the issue of the better, cheaper, longer gutta percha ball replacing the feathery—signaling another end of an era. "Progress" may now again be transforming golf, taking it in startling, unforeseen directions, making it more like other sports. No matter how quaint they may seem, these relationships with the past sustain and nourish golf.

Their mutual admiration a matter of record, less widely recognized is Jones's interest in Jack's future.

We know of one certifiable bit of direct advice conveyed with characteristic Jones dexterity, delivered second-hand to Jack's father who naturally passed it on to Jack. "I think I was a fairly good young golfer," Bob Jones wrote Charlie (they were on a first-name basis) "but I never became what I would call a really good golfer until I had been competing for quite a number of seasons." He relayed how at the first sign of swing trouble, he'd "run home" to Stewart Maiden back at East Lake. "Finally," he said, "I matured to the point where I understood my game well enough to make my own corrections...and *that's* when I'd say I became a *good* golfer." The parable—and the italics—were not lost on Jack. Uncomfortable with the tag of "best amateur since Bobby Jones" and the comparisons, he would later write, the story made "a particularly strong impression." On rare occasions in life the timing is right. As happened this time with Jack, he had the wherewithal to take the advice to heart.

In addition to the need to earn a living, Jack's decision to turn pro carried an additional benefit along with the obvious risk. To his relief he could abandon—once and for all—the direct record comparisons to Jones and the weighty expectations associated with it. As those in pursuit of legends learn, the chasing hard numbers can be stifling.

As he struggled with his decision to turn pro or remain an amateur, Jack heard from Bob Jones, the one person most sympathetic to his plight, and his father's boyhood idol. Jack's personal circumstances were different but Bob offered a unique perspective in appreciating Jack's dilemma. In *My Story*, Nicklaus says he received a "nice letter" from Jones suggesting he retain his amateur standing, but by then, with a seven-and-a-half week old son at home and two quarters left at Ohio State before getting his degree, he'd already made up his mind. Before he could change it, Charlie and his wife, Barbara, helped him find the words. It's fanciful to wonder whether Jack could've been swayed by the force of Jones's advocacy to remain an amateur golfer; that seems unlikely. In any event, the letter arrived too late to have any effect. Sadly, that letter seems to have vanished.

Jack tracked down USGA executive director Joe Dey in Florida, and over the telephone read him the letter they'd all worked on. During this eventful time, there was a flurry of correspondence back and forth between Charlie and Bob. Jack's pop had indeed hoped Jack would follow in his hero's footsteps. It was, however, all a moot point when Charlie wrote Bob Jones on Nicklaus Pharmacy stationery on November 9, 1961:

> I have always wanted Jack to remain an Amateur but never have tried to make a decision for him. But among other benefits, the desire to play golf on a near full time basis, being able to continue his insurance work, the several sources of income available to him made it seem rather unfair to his family not to decide as he did.

In his almost apologetic letter to Dey, Jack noted that composing it had not been a "pleasant chore." Dey understood and appreciated being kept informed. He wished Jack well. Looking back through the lens of hindsight, it's fascinating to imagine a player of his eventual accomplishment struggling with the decision to turn pro. All the majors and dramatics, of course, lay in the future. Fanciful, too, to consider how the landscape of the modern game might have been altered had the future Golden Bear remained an amateur. Forget for a moment the idea of an amateur winning six green jackets. For starters, what would've become of the Ryder Cup without Jack's insistence that Great Britain and Ireland expand their horizons to include Europe? And, what, too, would the golf world have been like without Jack's outstanding demonstration of sportsmanship in conceding Tony Jacklin's penultimate putt at the conclusion of the 1969 matches? Not to mention his worldwide success in course design.

Albeit "…with mixed emotions and considerable thought" he was now a professional golfer. "It would be unfair to my family not to accept this new responsibility," he wrote Dey. Jones would have been unable to find a more compelling argument.

The great amateur also understood, as he communicated to Charlie upon returning for an enjoyable mid-November visit to Augusta ("The golf course looks beautiful, and, I am even tempted to say, better than usual for this time of the year"). Jack's decision would in no way dampen his enthusiasm. Jones put in a good word on equipment maker Spalding's behalf. Maybe there could be "the pleasure of further association."

He closed the letter on November 16, 1961: "Whatever may be Jack's course from here out, I want you both to know that I shall continue to follow his career with considerable interest and that I shall always be hoping that he will have great success. Jack is a fine boy and a wonderful golfer who can do great things for the game."

Success would not be long in coming, nor confirmation of Jones's assertion. When Jack outdueled Arnold Palmer at Oakmont for the 1962 U.S. Open, oblivious to the gallery taunts from Arnie's Army, taunts of "Blobbo!" and worse, (enough to turn Charlie's neck red in silent fury), there was a letter from Jones stating how pleased he was with Jack's win, and a confession. "I like and admire Palmer very much, but still Mary and I were glued to the television set pulling hard for Jack to win. I hope you will congratulate Jack for both of us." A curling, dastardly putt that Nicklaus needed to save par on the 17th hole on Saturday—a jam job that succeeded—was hit so hard, Jones wrote to Charlie, "that I nearly jumped out of my chair." Jones wanted to know what Jack was thinking. Charlie relayed the answer, as Jack was off to Troon: "He said only somebody that could understand the entire situation, such as yourself, would have picked that particular putt."

When Charlie Nicklaus passed away on February 19, 1970, Jones sent a lovely note of condolence. And when Jack received an honorary degree from St. Andrews University in 1984, having served as a board member for the Jones Trust, a student exchange between Emory and St. Andrews, he paid Jones tribute. He referred to him as having been a "very special person in my life and an inspiration to all who had an opportunity to know him."

For six years preceding his own death, starting in 1964, Jones's most frequent pen pal was the irrepressible Gene Sarazen, then traveling the world hosting the *Shell Wonderful World of Golf* shows. Needless to say it is hard to imagine Tiger Woods and ....oh, say, Phil Mickelson, in their dotage maintaining a warm, regular correspondence. But that was then, and Sarazen and Jones shared an understanding and a wealth of shared life experience.

On top of the obvious mutual respect, despite the dramatic differences in their upbringings, their friendship is easily explained. They genuinely liked each other. "I couldn't say enough about Bobby Jones," Sarazen later reflected. "He was such a gentleman. I always got a thrill when I was paired with him in the Open and they paired me quite a few times with him."

Sarazen came from very different circumstances, far removed from the Southern privilege of the "Athens of the South" that shaped Jones's upbringing. A golfer deemed a triumph of "perspiration over inspiration," Gene never forgot the early poverty; his mother sending him out to pluck dandelions so there'd be something to put in the soup. His life in golf, he reflected, had allowed him to know the "rich side of it and I was the poor side of it." Not surprisingly, he was not in Jones's league as a correspondent; few could be. Gene's handwritten letters are replete with spelling and grammatical errors, often penned on the run on hotel stationary at odd hours, but the missives arrived regularly from all points of the compass, engaging travelogues always with a congenial, upbeat tone, even when the going got rough. "The apple crop looks light but healthy," he typically ended one letter from his upstate New York home following up a visit in Atlanta, ending, as always, "Give my very best to your Mary." Both men were married to Marys.

"We liked each other," Sarazen explained the friendship to oral historian Alice Kendrick, eight years before his death at the age of 97, in 1999. "We liked what we represented." Jones's less frequent replies would catch up with Gene eventually. Jones was a "faithful follower" of the Shell shows. Alongside Sarazen, he filmed a cameo when Sam Snead and Julius Boros came to town for a match at Peachtree that aired in February 1967. Jones was not pleased with his on-camera performance, however. He regretted not having found "something a bit more gracious to say to Sam and Julius," and went so far as to write Shell's public relations head Gordon Biggar. He also suggested culling a Sarazen comment that implicated Jack Nicklaus for his slow pace of play. The two greats had talked on camera about the modern scourge of slow play, and Jack's name had come up. "This is a valid point," Jones wrote the Squire back at his Mountain Range Farm in upstate New York, "and should be made for the good of the game." But. "There is no need to single out any one player, and I feel certain that you would not want to do this."

Gene agreed and saw to it. "You can rest assured," he wrote back, "that nothing will go on the air without your approval."

When necessary, Jones was not reluctant to go to bat for his old friend. Shell co-host George Rodgers clearly didn't know much about golf and his showmanship grated or Sarazen, who was awkward enough before the camera without having to deal with being upstaged by a golf neophyte. After hearing from his friend, Jones took the liberty of writing the head of Shell Oil about Rodgers. Sure, he was an "attractive personality," Jones conceded, but "I also think that his sometimes breathless commentary would be better suited to a horse race or a prize fight than to a leisurely contest at golf. In short, I should like to hear a good deal more of Sarazen on the program, and I have encountered many, many others who share my view." After numerous minor imbroglios, including Rodgers repeated influence in seeing Sarazen sequences end up on the cutting room floor, replaced with his own, Rodgers finally went too far and was fired.

Mostly, though, the letters were just good road stories: an unwelcome episode of the Mexican "trots," camels, the allure of Paris, sight seeing, a spiral of cocktail parties and some of the world's most exotic golf courses. Things got a lot lighter when Jimmy Demaret signed on. The three-time Masters champion, a jovial sort, was quick on his feet and not averse to enjoying himself. A couple of drinks, by the Squire's estimation, and Jimmy would start singing. He'd also known the poor side of golf having come up through the caddie yard. Of course, his golfing chops were substantial and he was a born entertainer. They got along beautifully and Sarazen appreciated the quick Demaret wit. It was Jimmy who once suggested the show might be more appropriately titled "Shell's Wonderful World of Parties." At one such affair, the wife of the governor of the Virgin Islands seemed confused by Sarazen's presence, and unsure of the show's purpose. She wanted to know if any pretty girls were involved, and what he had to do with it. He wrote Jones that he told her he carried the cameras.

Among the more memorable visits was a trip to martially-controlled Burma. The good will trip on the insistence of the state department featured crowds greeting his arrival and departure at two in the morning. The heat was as oppressive as the grueling schedule of exhibitions, matches, and diplomatic functions. The golf was interesting, though, and the people friendly. "It was the greatest experience I ever had," he wrote back, this despite miserable greens. There was also the novel discovery of a six-foot long deadly viper coiled around one of the holes. After it was dispatched, various spots on the golf course were pointed out to him as likely home to cobra nests. "Lovely place," he deadpanned from Athens.

Jones enjoyed the vicarious visits, and read the letters to his wife. After the Burma letter (with a photo of the adventurer wrapped in a sarong), his reply caught up with Sarazen at the Campo de Golf club in Madrid. "We are both so very happy that you are having all these interesting experiences," he wrote. "In effect, you have made a new career for yourself, and I am sure you must be getting a real bang out of it."

Madrid, Oslo, Manila, Rome, Paris, Athens, Caracas, Turnberry, Osaka, each week in season brought a new regular stream of adventures and handwritten installments on hotel stationery. When the luster started to dull, Jones was quick to recognize the irony of the world traveler.

"The first paragraph of your letter amuses me a bit," he wrote in July 1967. "I think you wrote me the same thing last year; that is, that you were so happy to be back on the farm. But in a week or so, you wrote me that you were getting a little bit fed up with the quiet life. I am expecting this time that the old war horse will get the same smell of gunpowder and want to be on the road again."

The old war horse, with his Old Rarity at his side, was capable of great things. "You would be surprised at what the human body will endure," he wrote at 4 a.m. from Japan, "especially if you have a good brand of whiskey like Old Rarity." His glowing enthusiasm for the single malt eventually prompted Jones to take the plunge. He liked it all right but questioned paying an extra $15 a case.

Later that year, Gene was on familiar ground to both men, ensconced in the comfort of Rusack's Hotel in St. Andrews, looking out over the Old Course. "I could almost see hell bunker at a distance and my mind turns back 34 years ago, when I took eight on that 14th hole only to lose the title by one stroke. Thousands of people are roaming the course. It's Sunday and the Old Course is closed. I hope you enjoy these short notes as much as I enjoy sitting down and reliving some of the past when you and I were young. O Boy."

When the road started to get old, Jones was quick with a kind word. From Venezuela, a difficult shoot, the anti-American sentiment obvious, and where Demaret was detained, Sarazen couldn't help adding a weary postscript: "I am afraid the end of all my activities are near." Jones wouldn't hear of it. "I do not take the last paragraph of your letter seriously," he replied. "I cannot imagine that you will ever come to the end of your "activities." Sarazen was then 67 years old.

Christmas of 1969, Gene sent an extra crate of apples from the farm, and was assured they were "enjoyed to the fullest." There was always the Masters to look forward to. Jones wrote: "...I hope to be quite in form to receive you."

It was not to be. "I had hopes of seeing you," Sarazen wrote a week

135
•

after the tournament, "but I was informed by Cliff the trip was more than you could take. The Masters dinner was very quiet. Hogan came up and left the next morning. The weather was beautiful throughout. You would have loved the greens, just perfect, the fairways show the sign of a hard winter. It was by far the greatest tournament ever. We keep saying this every year."

An informal anniversary arrived, not unnoticed. It had been 50 years since the two first met, at the 1920 U.S. Open at Inverness, in Toledo. Jones was then 20, the youngest player in the field. Sarazen finished seventeen shots behind Edward Ray, resolving afterwards to address inconsistencies in his game. Jones fared better, tying for 8th place, four shots back. Two years later, Gene would win the Open, clipping Jones and fellow amateur John L. Black by a stroke. Time was marching on. After nine years the Shell shows had run their course. He'd put the New York farm up for sale. The Squire would divide his time between Marco Island, Florida and summer at a new place in New Hampshire. Gene hadn't played well at the Masters but was in good shape and planning to go over for the 1970 British Open at St. Andrews. "I'll think of you when walking down those rugged fairways," he wrote his old friend. At the Masters, Bob's son, Bob Jones III, had invited Gene down to the cabin for a drink. He'd promised he'd make it, but he couldn't. "It's an empty cabin without you and Mary," he closed out the last letter in the USGA collection. If there was a reply, it's not in the file. Jones died less than two years later, on December 18th, 1971. In the ensuing years when passing through Atlanta, the old war horse would pull sportswriter Furman Bisher along and they'd go out to Oakland Cemetery and pay their respects, Gene leaving wreaths on the graves of Mr. & Mrs. Jones.

five

• • • • d e a r m s .
s o r e n s t a m • • • •

The press room was deserted. No one but the cleaning crew finishing their rounds, certainly no reporters or tournament officials. Not at this hour. The bomb sniffing dogs wouldn't swing through for another hour. The place was as quiet as the darkened television at the front of the room. Six in the morning and it had already been a miserable day. The topper was still a couple of hours off.

Up well before dawn, I drove over to the upscale Fort Worth neighborhood and parked in a private home's driveway near enough to Colonial Country Club to walk. The parking space had been secured the previous evening at a cut rate ($25) as I figured to be gone by Noon. I passed through the quiet streets on foot in pitch darkness to the stately club entrance. Stopping periodically to rest my arms from carrying the broadcast equipment, I paused at the Hogan statue, then made my way down the stairs and onto the deserted grounds. Not a soul or a sound was to be heard. I followed my nose around shadowy landmarks to the brick indoor tennis center converted for the week into media facilities. The door to the media center would be open at 5 a.m., I'd been assured. No worries. Of course it was locked as my pessimist instincts were certain it would be, just as sure as the door proved immune to my pathetic banging. The first of several rushing streams of panic and anger subsided before I groped my way around the building and found an open side door. After a sleepless night, the walk lugging the heavy equipment, and my childish drum rolls against the door, sweat was now freely flowing down my sides. My heart was pounding. If I wasn't before, I was wide awake now.

The radio station's remote equipment was supposed to be foolproof. Maybe so. Most technology, I've found, only responds to those who know how to use it, a fatal defect. Days before, the engineer walked me through the shiny red box's instructions. The cord goes here, the phone line here and here. What could be easier? I took notes. The box I knew would test out fine. Of course it fired right up in the press room on Friday afternoon, with help from a tech-savvy friend. But today was Saturday and I was alone.

In the back of my mind was my previous experience with the shiny red box. Live from the PGA Merchandise Show in Orlando, several years before, for 45 minutes, every word out of my mouth disturbingly echoed in my headphones, a private hellish glitch as only I could hear it. This, I later learned, was not my fault. An inexperienced producer back at the station had let me down, not for the first time. Skillful producers have for no other reason than their professionalism worked hard for years to make me look and sound good. There have been exceptions. The grand pooba was "Loopy." Loopy made me sympathize with Margaret Dumont, the old dowager of the Marx Brothers movies who ruined her insides trying to maintain a straight face against their absurdity. Someday I may have an ulcer named Loopy. The anxiety of not knowing what was coming next in working with this man formed a growing pit in my gut as my radio show on Saturday morning approached. It could be anything.

Loopy routinely passed the time by removing his cowboy boots and smoldering socks. Kicking back, just out of reach from me on the other side of the console, he'd commence picking his feet. Had I been hit in the face with a cream pie, it wouldn't have as completely derailed my train of thought. Only once had it ever been as bad. My first job in radio was "ripping and reading" the news on a small Vermont AM station in the mornings before going to class. "Big John," the disc jockey, went about 5' 9", 275 pounds. Each weekday morning from 6 to 10 he consumed a six-pack of Coke. When he was feeling particularly vindictive, he'd stroll over to the front of my glassed-in booth and wait for me to garble some-one's name. If I was proficiently reading the copy, he'd make his move: a favorite was stuffing two elongated tissues in his nostrils. He'd then sud-denly appear at the window, performing a vigorous dance jumping up and down and screaming. As he was on the other side of the thick, sound-proofed glass, the performance was solely for my benefit. When I'd com-pletely lost it, which never took long, he'd retreat, satisfied, back to the demands of the board and the next record or commercial.

But these were deliberate acts. Loopy was oblivious, which somehow made it worse. Once he inexplicably deserted his post as a caller was fin-ishing up making his remarks on the air. The caller made his point. I thanked him. He hung up the phone. That's pretty much how talk radio goes. This time the dial tone was immediate, followed seconds later by the disarming sequence of piercing tones. I then heard a familiar voice delivering comments wholly unrelated to golf. "If you'd like to make a call…," she said. All this went out over the air. For years incidents such as these led me resignedly to conclude that, more often than not, what was happening on my side of the microphone was far more entertaining than what was going out over the air. Recalling these nightmares still quickens the pulse. Fortunately, as they say with radio: in one ear and out the other.

Annika Sorenstam's historic 2003 appearance on the PGA Tour was big news and it brought me up to Fort Worth, Cowtown. To commemorate the occasion, I'd been deeded an extra hour for a special two-hour edition of That's Golf! on KVET-AM in Austin. The week started promisingly. I followed the tight smiling Swede around the golf course, drank in the charged atmosphere on the 10th tee, her first, on Thursday, attended the press conferences and did numerous *phone-ins* back to the all-sports station. The week also featured my first television stand-up. Nearly soaked through from the inevitable humidity in my blazer and tie, Sportsnet viewers in Canada must have wondered what had come over the correspondent shortly after he'd been brought on the air. Just as the finger pointed to me to signify I was live, a rivulet of chilled rainwater from a freshening thunderstorm rolled off a canopy and trickled down my back. Whatever happened after that is a blur.

For the radio show (8 to 10 a.m.) I asked *New York Times* columnist Dave Anderson to join me. The author of one of my favorite boxing books, *In the Corner*, is a winner of the PGA Lifetime Achievement Award in Journalism. He would be on his way out of town Saturday morning, he said. Despite a credible performance, Annika missed the cut and the story was over. Colonial reverted back to being just a golf tournament. Her press conferences that week had been celebratory affairs, absolutely jammed, as big as at any major. In the partitioned room one over from Annika, a few lone reporters would bravely visit with those who were merely playing well enough to lead the tournament. If West Texas boy and rising star Chad Campbell was disappointed to find only myself, Phil Wooddall, who handled sports for an Amarillo station and had known Campbell since he was a sprout, and Jimmy Burch from the *Star-Telegram*, to talk to after he posted his second 67, he never let on.

Anderson said sure, he'd do it. I'd also lined up Jack Whitaker. Not bad, I thought. A Pulitzer Prize winner and a legendary sports presence who likes to tell stories. Jack was also a winner of the Lifetime Achievement Award. Whitaker had recently come out with a tweedy remembrance, *Preferred Lies and Other Tales*, and there was plenty of golf in it. He couldn't have been nicer. I'd read his book, reviewed it favorably, and naturally had a soft spot as a Philadelphian for the former stentorian voice of the Philadelphia Eagles. He assured me he'd be ready. I didn't mention it but years before I'd arrived at the bar of our family's favorite New York restaurant, Geno's, to find my mother chatting amiably with a stranger. It was none other than Whitaker. She had no idea who he was.

Very pleased with myself I'd taken the liberty of alerting the drive-time shows at the radio station who, I'd hoped, in exchange for free live reports, would plug my upcoming Saturday show and the very special guests. Despite all its history, Colonial had been having trouble attracting a strong field and competing against the hard-charging charitable Salesmanship Club army associated with Byron Nelson's tournament in Irving. Sorenstam's presence had obviously given the event a shot in the arm. The crowds were upbeat, well supplied with the churnings from the ubiquitous margarita machines, and almost entirely in her corner. She'd wisely picked a course that would accentuate her accuracy, where her shorter length off the tee would not put her at, she hoped, an insurmountable disadvantage.

At least early in the week, the media was just as giddy as the crowds. There were 'Go Annika' buttons and a festive atmosphere. As a freelancer I'd ended up in the very back of the large working area, which was fine as I didn't spend much time there. Seated next to a Danish news correspondent who'd never covered golf, I was extensively interviewed.

As the minutes ticked closer to airtime on Saturday morning, my desperation intensified. Despite my best efforts, it became clear that the connection with the station could not be made. For nearly two hours I'd tried with the futility of a downed pilot calling MAYDAY from a perch in the South Pacific. Since the phone I was trying to connect the ISBN line, or whatever it's called, was 15 feet away from the bank of courtesy phones I was using to talk to a human voice in Austin, I had to wander back and forth to communicate with a befuddled producer. The fall back was to just go with the courtesy media phone and feed that right over the air. The sound quality would suffer but if the connection wouldn't work, it was that or nothing. For two hours, I'd have to wing it. I couldn't leave my post during station breaks for fear that someone would wander by and simply hang up the stray receiver. The restrooms were too far away to risk.

Soon enough it was showtime! The Anderson interview has been erased from my memory. I seem to recall that it went smoothly. He was where he said he'd be. We chatted. He answered my questions. His cell phone worked. I could hear him. He could hear me. So far so good. Those arriving to the slowly awakening press room would be greeted by a man literally shouting through a courtesy phone over by the fax machines. I kept my back turned, did my best, and tried to pretend that this wasn't happening.

I wasn't nearly so lucky with Whitaker. We took our break at the top of the hour. I always prepare for the worst, the inevitable news—30 seconds before going back on the air—that the guest is not on the other end, or he thought the interview was scheduled for next week, or he's doing his nails. The show had been heavily promoted; I kept my fingers crossed, planning to go to Plan B. Lo and behold, word came down the line that we had Jack! Good to go.

I introduced him as coolly (without overdoing it) as a man, up at four in the morning who hadn't eaten and been screaming and banging on a locked door, could in shouting through the receiver. As hard as it was for me to hear myself, once removed without the benefit of technology, the sound would be even worse for someone on another line—a point of diminishing returns with each connection. I'm guessing. In any event the quality was so poor that my ear had to be crammed so far into the receiver it would need to be peeled off. Jack was getting up in years and his hearing might not have been terrific to start with. It was not helped by a crappy connection. I plugged Jack's book and started in. As best as I can recall, most of the 10 to 12 minute interview, live, without a break, went something like this:

> ME: Jack Whitaker's my guest. Jack, thank you very much for joining me. I'm here at Colonial in Fort Worth where Ben Hogan won a record five National Invitational titles. His presence, like the statue at the club's entrance, still stands sentinel over the game, especially here. What first comes to mind when you think back on Hogan?
> JACK WHITAKER: What? Jim, are you there? I can't hear your question.
> ME: (agitation evident, Louder): What comes to mind when...you
> think of... BEN HOGAN?
> WHITAKER: Hogan did what now?
> ME: (frantic, yelling) About BEN...HOGAN!!
> WHITAKER: I can't hear a thing. What's that you say about Hogan?

That may have been one of the more lucid exchanges. A nightmare, basically. The only thing that could have made it worse, in retrospect, would've been the timing. Players are on the golf course relatively early on the weekend. The leaders don't tee off until afternoon, and the press typically follows the leaders. Had this played out before an *in-studio* audience on Friday afternoon, rather than early on Saturday morning, I'd probably have gently replaced the receiver, saddled up, headed straight over to Angelo's for several schooners of frosty iced adult refreshment and some barbecue and never looked back.

Mercifully, the show finally ended. I'd had enough and was headed home, relieved to be walking against the grain of those streaming in the gate. Packing up I noticed a fax sitting in a tray. I couldn't help myself. It was a letter addressed to Sorenstam c/o of her agent, and dated Wednesday, the 21st of May when Annika excitement was peaking.

"Dear Ms. Sorenstam," it began:

"Some people you will be playing with are gentlemen. Some are not."

That was it. The letter was signed, "Regards, Bill Cosby." I wonder if she ever got it. Probably not, since it was just gathering dust in the press room. If she did see it, I wonder if she had any idea who he was.

• • • • • t h e s h o t h e a r d ' r o u n d t h e b l o c k • • • •

By the time Gene Sarazen holed his improbable double-eagle en route to winning the 1935 Masters—his Wilson Jim Gallagher Turf Rider giving as advertised in the catalog, "a marvelous account of itself on use through the fairway"—another shot that he once declared "the greatest... I ever played in my life and the greatest I ever expect to play," was history. That time he wielded a wedge not a 4-wood. Sarazen's opponent, an English professional named Fred Robson, called it the best shot he'd seen in thirty years of golf.

"You will be reading of it or avoiding repetitious stories of it for years to come," Westbrook Pegler tipped off readers in the *Chicago Tribune*. It was a "happening, like the home run that stuck in the knothole and the bouncing dropkick that jumped over the Princeton goal."

Even before his immortal dramatics at the Masters four years later, Sarazen's equally-masterful shot was destined for obscurity. Along with the bouncing dropkick and the knotholed homer, the "miracle shot" that "astounded the gallery" would be Wally Pipped, topped by his own brilliance, and, now, 75 years later all but forgotten.

There was just cause. Some accounts of the match, including Alan Gould's Associated Press reports, neglected to mention it. Nor did it appear in the account written up by a newly-retired Bobby Jones who attended the matches.

It took place during a Ryder Cup though the circumstances weren't especially noteworthy. A U.S. victory was anticipated on both sides of the Atlantic that year and the U.S. won in a rout. In the weeks prior to the start of the matches, famed sportswriter Grantland Rice nevertheless gave it the old college try, cautioning against over-confidence.

"It might be remembered," he wrote *In the Sportlight* two weeks before play got underway, "that the British have had the better of all match-play tests in which even as fine a player as Hagen has had more than his share of trouble." He needn't have worried. Captain Hagen, bronzed and cocky, was spectacular. No less a connoisseur than Henry Cotton lamented "Walter's almost heartbreaking" accuracy. His team was no less formidable. Newcomer Billy Burke (Burkauskus), 29, was magnificent, besting Jones' winning 1926 score on the same course in leading team qualifying. Burke continued his sterling play, under par for both rounds of his 36-hole singles match in defeating veteran Archie Compston. In a 72-hole challenge match in 1928, Compston had famously vanquished Sir Walter 18 and 17. Burke, exceptionally straight from tee to green despite the loss of the two small fingers on his left hand, would follow up his dazzling performance weeks later by winning the U.S. Open, contested due to playoffs over a marathon 144 holes.

Few of the matches were close, as the U.S. jumped out to a commanding 3-1 lead. "The British Lion found the beak and talons of the American Eagle a trifle too robust in the first day's test..." Rice informed his readers. Bernard Darwin's post mortem (he was not there) would be tinged with thinly-veiled annoyance. The eventual 9-3 blowout, he concluded, "can hardly be surprising except to those who regard it as a patriotic duty to expect what they know will not happen."

Unlike the illustrious double-eagle, this miraculous shot did not swing momentum or court destiny. Did it result in a double-eagle? Not exactly. Well, then, an eagle. No. A birdie? Nope. It didn't even result in a par. In stroke play it would've been an outstanding bogey but match play is a series of individual contests; stroke play the best cumulative result over four days. The shot came early in Sarazen's singles match with Robson and had no effect on the result. Gene bogeyed the hole losing it to a routine par. He was three-up at the time and went on to win his point with ease, 7 and 6. What's more, oddly enough, the remarkable shot may have been trumped within minutes, not even the most spectacular play that day *on that same hole!*

Adding to the confusion, nearly every press account that highlighted the brilliant save got something about it wrong. Sarazen didn't help matters. His own retelling of the "happening" only further muddied the waters. *The Sunday Times* had him somehow playing off a roof. It was nothing like that. Actually, what happened was. . .well, we'll come to it.

Before the 1931 matches began, two events conspired to overshadow and additionally ensure the brave shot's obscurity.

The matches were held in Columbus, Ohio, at Scioto Country Club, the site of the 1926 U.S. Open won by Bobby Jones. His every shot would be watched admiringly by a 13-year old who, in his son's later estimation, "lived, talked and slept sports," and would come to worship the great amateur and all he represented. An 11-letter man at Columbus South High, Charlie Nicklaus played number one on the golf team and later also played some semi-pro football before settling down to run his pharmacies. He joined Scioto and took up golf to recover from ankle surgery. It was there that his 10-year old son Jack, also a good young athlete, would grip a golf club for the first time.

There had been some problems in 1926, and four of the creeping Columbia bent grass greens had been replaced. If golf writers hacking their way around the course just prior to the matches are to be believed, the greens were in better shape. The tassel grass rough, poetically described by one as, "that waxy Midwest growth with silken whiskers which billows with the pleasant sheen of a prayer rug, but snares the irons and turns the blades when..full grown," was down. It was still "very rough," but not as bad as when Jones overtook Joe Turnesa. A long course, playing to 6,745 yards, golfing Britons were told to expect "a very fair if not over-exacting test of golf."

There is a story, perhaps apocryphal, about the rough in that 1926 championship. And they complain about today's second-cut. How high was it at Scioto? So high that Bill Mehlhorn recalled losing his fellow competitor, the diminutive Scottish-expatriate with the marvelous name of Bobby Cruickshank, in it. Variously estimated at somewhere between 5' 1" and 5' 6," 'Cruicky' was a former member of the famed Black Watch regiment during the First World War, twice seeing heavy action and a P.O.W. A fine golfer, he won 17 tournaments in the U.S., and very nearly a U.S. Open, finishing second twice in the PGA Championship. He later settled in Florida.

Cruickshank disappeared into the rough in search of an errant drive.

"Cruicky," Mehlhorn called out, "where are you?"

"Here I am, Bill" came a voice. It wasn't until Cruickshank waved a club over his head that his friend could locate him amidst the thick undergrowth. Well, you know… The story, however, may bear more than a grain of truth. Bob Jones shared the story of his caddie nearly losing his clubs in the tall rough after setting down the bag to assist another player in finding his ball.

So the British team set sail for America on June 10th with all the prospects of the Light Brigade. A series of matches in New York and Boston awaited them before making their way to Ohio. The commanding Compston led the early morning "gymnastic parade," while less energetic members strolled the decks before breakfast stretching their legs. Team manager Fred Pignon, in his dual role as correspondent, assured the home front that the team left for Columbus "optimistic and determined."

They also left England dogged by controversy characterized as "insane," and an "imbecility." Described as "has-beens," "damned and despairful," they were assured by most observers of a "gallant and pathetic defeat," a "golfing Moscow."

A rules technicality—with heaping spoonfuls of ego and indignancy mixed in—guaranteed that three of Great Britain's best would not play. The rule, in force for both sides, was that all players be natives of the country they represent. They must also be employed and live there. That was the problem. Expatriate Britons had long flocked to America to seek their fortune in the game, most notably Tommy Armour and, "the human one iron," Jim Barnes. It was a clause that the British PGA and Ryder Cup benefactor Samuel Ryder staunchly defended, and it would unfairly penalize at least one naturalized American, Harry "Light Horse" Cooper, from representing his adopted country. Cooper was guilty only of the heinous offense of arriving in the States as a toddler.

The "invaders" desperately needed Percy Alliss and Aubrey Boomer on the team, but both made their livings on the continent. Henry

T. H. COTTON

Cotton, a pro at 17 and already a star in his early 20s, and the hero of the 1929 matches at Moortown, would also not be on the side. Boomer, based in Paris, had just won another of his eventual five French Opens, with a final round 67. Alliss lived in Berlin. He, too, with Cotton, would enjoy a lengthy and distinguished career, leaving Scioto as a spectator to nearly best a stellar field at the Canadian Open. By the end of the year, Alliss bid Germany adieu, citing the "call of home," and the wish for his sons to have a British education.

By then, of course, it was too late to do anything about the 1931 result. Alliss would play three times for King and country in the Ryder Cup compiling a winning record before World War II's intercession. His prodigal golfing son, Peter, would follow and succeed him with an exceptional eight appearances.

Cotton would go on to win three Open championships. He would also return to the fold, twice more as a Ryder Cup player and twice as captain. He journeyed to Columbus, like Jones, to lend his expertise in covering the competition, and, so he averred, make himself available at the last minute should the PGA relax their demands. That did not happen.

His beef was more personal, a matter played out in the press with upstanding decorum worthy of the Marquis of Queensbury. Cotton and PGA secretary Percy T. Perrins issued formal salvos back and forth before an exasperated golfing public and press.

"There is nobody more patriotic than myself," Cotton defended himself in *Golf Illustrated*, "and there is nobody who appreciates the great honour of playing for one's country more than I do. But I do feel that, no matter how patriotic one is, one cannot be true to one's country if one does not rest true to oneself."

Refined and independent, Cotton was the first notable exception to the rule of the subservient British club professional. He preferred to travel as he wished at his own expense, play exhibitions wherever he chose, on his own time, returning to England when he felt like it. The British PGA insisted he travel with the team coming and going and pool all earnings. He refused. That was that. No Cotton for England.

The three outcasts, accompanied by French golfer Auguste Boyer, and Cotton's brother, Leslie, had a "most enjoyable crossing" on the S.S. Europa, (no mention of their gymnastic regimen). His presence at the matches an obvious thorn to British golf officials, Cotton couldn't resist politely rubbing it in, sharing with his readers the novelty of donning a press armband, sporting an open collar and carrying his umbrella, wandering "hither and thither listening to the remarks of the spectators whilst watching the various matches."

If there was any enmity between those players representing their country and those merely in attendance, it did not make the papers. "The British team is partly composed of people whom no one in this country has ever heard of," chided Pegler. The same charge has been true through the years, of course, and on numerous occasions has proven a source of unwise and unmerited Yankee overconfidence. Not this time.

Without the two young stars, and Boomer, by then a seasoned international, even Cotton, at his civil best, could hardly have taken any delight in assessing the team's chances. When the result was in, the Americans entertaining themselves with rousing versions of college songs, Cotton wrote back that "I am afraid it was expected that we should lose the cup."

One of those gallant old war horses on the British side was Fred Robson, then 46, more acclaimed for his skills as an instructor and clubmaker than player. He'd had a nice run, once finishing second (six shots back) in the Open to Bob Jones at St. Andrews in 1927, with two fourth place finishes, the last at Hoylake, in 1930. He'd once beaten Hagen in an exhibition at his home course in the south of England (Hagen received twenty pounds more), but all that was in the past. Darwin would later eulogize him as a "fine upstanding player with a style both graceful and powerful…with a wonderfully keen eye for the strengths and weaknesses of the styles of others."

·   The severest criticism of the British side was reserved for 1920 Open champion Duncan. Once renowned for his remarkable speed of play, the 48-year old Scot had lost his groove. The consensus was that he would have far better served the team from the sidelines. Fans, noted one scribe, felt sorry for him, "with no distance from the tee, and a putter bobbling the ball up and down on the green and never looking like holing a putt." Robson and Duncan's combined ages, American John Anderson wrote in the British *Golf Illustrated*, "were something not to be spoken of except in whispers." Funny how things go. These days Presidents and Ryder Cup teams are routinely filled with "seasoned" players over-40 who have performed quite capably, valued for their experience.

For the first day's foursomes, the old timers stole a point. Robson was paired with another legendary early twentieth century luminary, Abe Mitchell, then 44, perhaps the first great player dogged by the odious title of 'best never to win a major [the Open].' Cotton later wrote, in an otherwise affectionate profile, that Mitchell lacked the killer instinct, "his gentlemanly, reserved disposition…" preventing him "from ruthlessly driving home an advantage. Abe was beaten now and then by players who had no right to defeat him." The veterans rallied to secure the only point for their team on the opening day, beating Al Espinosa and Leo Diegel 3 and 1 after being two-down after 18 holes.

The British were additionally vexed (and they believed hampered) by having to play the new, larger American ball. The more serious complication, however, was the weather. It was murderously hot that June in the Midwest. Records were repeatedly smashed. Red Wing, Minnesota topped out at 106 on the first day of the Ryder Cup. Nebraska had five successive days above 100 degrees. Aside from two brief squalls, there

Perhaps the first of the modern era greats to bear the unfortunate "best never to win a major" label, Abe Mitchell.

was little relief. Chicago recorded temperatures at 10 p.m. of 91 degrees. Fifty deaths were attributed to the heat on that day alone, Saturday, June 27th, with severe crop damage reported throughout the region.

The visitors couldn't take it. Pegler caught a glimpse of Duncan laid out on a bench in the locker room, his "compatriots gathered about him, shutting off the ventilation to fan him with their hats as though he had been a bowl of (sic) chile."

A month ago they'd been wearing leather jackets at Carnoustie. Here they melted, developing blisters, running through by Pignon's estimate four or more shirts a day, "saturated rags in a few moments." Some players, he said, lost 12 pounds. "We could not eat. Fruit, milk and cold chicken with an occasional egg were practically the only things taken for meals. ...Sleep was impossible." He'd cabled back to England for prescriptions and a masseur, to little effect. They'd been forewarned their stomachs couldn't handle ice. Pignon later wrote the situation got so dire that the team even sampled the ignoble American creation of iced tea. To no avail, it and lemonade "were unsuitable and milk and a sandwich was the most the players could take at mid-day." Pignon later adamantly defended his team criticizing those who had made them, to his mind, the "victims of abuse." In a widely circulated editorial column, he complimented the U.S. (a "team of supermen") but stressed the heat had decimated the ranks. He did agree with the critics on one point. "We shall never win a contest of this kind in the United States unless it is played in weather conditions which we can withstand."

The heat also deadened the crowds. Jones followed Hagen then sought shelter camping out anonymously under trees near the ninth and eighteenth greens. Cotton blamed the high ticket prices as much as the weather, but the PGA reported a profit. The visitors took the defeat in stride. "No better sports than the British Ryder cup team members have been seen in Columbus," wrote *Columbus Dispatch* columnist Frank Colley. "There wasn't a whimper when they lost, nothing but words of praise for their victorious opponents." Duncan admitted to Golfers Magazine's H.G. Salsinger that "We were beaten by much better golfers but there is no denying the new ball handicapped our play."

In his *American Post-Tournament Impressions*, for *Golfers Monthly*, Halford J. Morlan was more effusive towards the vanquished. "Never before in the history of international golf matches has a foreign team visited America and created such thoroughly sportsmanlike and genuinely friendly feelings as the recently defeated British Ryder Cup players." Sportsmanship carried the day with the noted exception of the only British journalist present, Trevor Wignall of the *Daily Express*, whom Cotton observed to be "so loyal and so patriotic that he became almost unpopular." Even *Golf Illustrated*, which took a hard line over the exclusion of Cotton, Alliss and Boomer, was conciliatory. "We have nothing but praise for the members of the British team." This would be the official line on what transpired over the "sun-baked plains" of Scioto. "The fact that their best was not good enough must not be counted against them."

The second singles match of the day featured Sarazen v. Robson. When they reached the fourth tee, Fred Robson was already three-down. The fourth hole at Scioto is the second longest of Donald Ross's four par-threes, then playing 180 yards. Fifteen yards to the left of the green rests a stone structure. Today it houses two restrooms and shades a couple of coolers of lemonade and iced water for the members. In 1931, it served as a refreshment stand. Sarazen with the honor hooked his two-iron off the tee. The ball bounded directly into the stand through the open window before coming to rest on a crack in the floor. Robson's ball found the green, stopping about twenty feet below the hole.

The hut, a hot dog stand, was filled with boxes of soda. The customer window measured six feet long by three feet wide, five feet off the floor. The dimensions were one of the few matters in general agreement.

"There is no point in building this story up," Pegler reported. "Sarazen flicked the ball from the floor to the green with his niblick, ten feet from the pin. Then he missed his putt and lost the hole with a four. There will be other versions of this curious incident. Already the story goes that Sarazen found the ball on a cake of ice and played it out with an ice pick." Francis Powers, western sports representative of the Consolidated Press, recapping the highlights for British readers, witnessed the shot. He noted that Sarazen hardly took any time to size up the situation and play. Several boxes were first carefully moved without disturbing the ball. Then the golfer, routinely described as the "stocky New Yorker," or "the squat Italian" (he was 5' 5"), gripped down on his niblick and pulled off the shot "with a strong flick of the wrist."

The *Columbus Dispatch* tracking each match hole-by-hole recorded that Sarazen's par putt from 10 feet missed by four inches. Robson lagged his first putt, then tapped in from two feet for the win, now two down after four holes. Sarazen made one brief aside about the shot. As both men scrambled to halve the next hole, the long par-four 5th, 445 yards long, he said his ball "must've been dry," that is, thirsty enough to seek out the pop stand.

That, however, is not the end of the story. In *Thirty Years of Championship Golf*, the hall of famer wrote that the fourth hole was the "turning point" in the match, that they'd been "moving along about the same speed," which implies the match was fairly close to that point. That was clearly not the case. Sarazen won the first three holes with a birdie and two pars against two bogeys and a double-bogey. He describes mov-

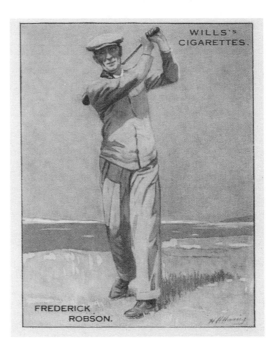

Eulogized by Henry Longhurst as "the family doctor of golf" for his teaching renown, Fred Robson had a tough Ryder Cup, though he got his par at the fourth.

ing a refrigerator out of the way with his caddie and playing the ball onto the green. Robson, he says, then "carelessly" three-putted from 25 feet. "I rolled my putt in for a 3," Sarazen wrote. "As we walked off the green, Fred surprised me by saying, "That was very tough luck, Gene."

"Fred, I had a 3, I answered.

"His face fell like a bride's first cake. "You did, Gene!" he exclaimed incredulously. "I thought you had an unplayable lie in the stand and had played a hand-mashie."

He goes on to write that the result "so disconcerted Fred" that he was effectively done, never playing another good shot the rest of the match.

For some reason this skewed version of events bugged me. I loved the story of the heroic recovery but somebody wasn't on the level. Every newspaper and magazine covering the event, whether they mentioned the shot or not, accurately had the hole score, if not the details. It was a great shot but three always beats four.

The authors couldn't have gotten this wrong. After several trips to the library and some thought on the matter, I decided to write Herb Wind, the book's coauthor. No impertinence was meant. Far be it for me to let the truth get in the way of a good story. My letter was suitably deferential and I was genuinely tickled when he took the time to respond.

Maturity takes most of us past the histrionics and the early attraction of the self-absorbed in sports to deeper levels of appreciation and respect. We all have our own guilty pleasures. Richie Allen, Joe Namath and Jimmy Connors thrilled this impressionable mind, later giving way to more sustaining heroes like Alan Page, Roberto Clemente and Arthur Ashe. A similar transformation has taken place with an attraction to the wry, less is more literary folks like Red Smith, Al Laney, Bill Lyon, Blackie Sherrod, Shirley Povich, and John McPhee, to name a few. So few graduates now remain from what might be termed, in tribute to the wisecracking TV talking horse, the Mr. Ed School of Broadcasting. A dying breed, those who, like *Ed*, went the theme song never spoke unless they have "something to say." Red Smith mordantly asserted that writing was easy. "All you have to do is sit down at the typewriter and open a vein." He would've found sports talk radio and color commentary even easier. All that has to be done is to sit down at a microphone and open a mouth. Discussing a play he'd written about Smith, biographer Ira Berkow said he hoped his one-time *New York Times* colleague left a legacy of "humor, perspective and an appreciation of language." Those are just the things that seem so lacking from sports coverage today.

Herbert Wind, of course, was a rare bird, a dinosaur, really, an essayist. Al Laney, another exceptional reporter, made this distinction between a columnist and an essayist. A columnist, he told Jerome Holtzman in *No Cheering in the Press Box*, tells us how to think whereas an essayist, who has room and license to ramble, tells us instead what he thinks. Wind's writings on golf are an intellectual delight with ample servings of humor, perspective and appreciation of language. Those patient enough to follow his elegant lead are rewarded, if, on any given Sunday we might have more fun with Henry Longhurst or Dan Jenkins.

Wind passed away in 2005. He once shared the pleasure of receiving a simply marked envelope each spring, an invitation from Bob Jones to stop by and visit during the Masters. His reply to my letter would be my equivalent, a simply marked envelope with a letter from the golf correspondent of *The New Yorker*—cool.

"Thank you for your interesting letter," he wrote on October 24, 1995. "I looked up the passage that you mention in "Thirty Years of Championship Golf." I finally found it on pages 202 and 203. [I'd already obviously read the original passage; otherwise, I'd never have heard about the shot, but I could let that go.] In short, Gene played his second off the cement floor of a refreshment stand behind the green and holed a ten-foot putt for a winning 3." As I'd already explained as courteously as I could, this was not so. Not then, not ever. "It's tucked away on pages 202-203 in "Thirty Years of Championship Golf." [Yes, sir. I know. That's why I was writing. Sorry to bother you. Just curious.] "Yours very truly, Herbert Warren Wind."

Oh well. Still, it was a great shot even if the putt didn't drop. Johnny Farrell also generated some excitement on the fourth hole that day. His iron fully cleared the refreshment stand and he was forced to pitch over the hut and a back bunker to have any chance of staying in the hole. To the delight of the gallery, he nearly holed out his pitch. With a 20-footer for the win, and his opponent's ball less than a foot from the cup, W.H. Davies found himself partially stymied. His bold attempt for birdie struck Farrell's ball knocking it in the cup for an unbelievable two! The unpredictable nature of the stymie in the days before marking and lifting balls on the green never had a more unexpected result. Imagine what must have been going through his mind. After each man's tee shot Davies seemed certain to win the hole. Unlike the Sarazen/Robson match, this one was in fact very close. Davies started the hole two-up. He was able to recover from the shock, however. He responded by winning the next two holes and turned it on in the afternoon to secure his point, 4 and 3. "These two shots were the talk of the big galleries all day long," wrote Rice.

For the record, it also wasn't true that Robson played as badly as Gene let on. A sub headline in afternoon editions of the *Columbus Citizen* blared: "Sarazen-Robson Battle Proves Exciting, Briton Making Surprisingly Accurate Recoveries After Bad Tee Shots." OK, Sarazen was four-up after the first 18 holes but in match play, you never know. As it turned out, Gene easily took down Robson, who later returned to the states in an official capacity, accompanying the 1949 Walker Cup team to Winged Foot just a few years before his death in 1952. And, incidentally, the niblick used to extricate himself from the pop stand was not the fabled sand wedge.

After the matches, the teams went their separate ways: the British to play exhibitions against a team of Michigan pros, the U.S. to Cincinnati. The big writers moved on after the matches to Cleveland for a heavyweight fight between Germany's Max Schmeling and Georgian Bill Stribling. Then it was over to Toledo for the U.S. Open, the first since Bobby Jones' retirement after winning the Grand Slam. It was an event John Kieran figured in *The New York Times* was something like "Hamlet without the Prince of Denmark." Rice still had golf on his mind. He drew an intriguing comparison between the title fight and the "big show at Toledo" to follow; a point that doesn't get raised nearly enough in considering the difficulties of major championship golf.

> Stribling has only to beat Schmeling. Schmeling has only to beat Stribling. The winner at Inverness must beat Armour, Mac Smith, Walter Hagen, Gene Sarazen, Henry Cotton, Wiffy Cox, Leo Diegel, Denny Shute, Archie Compston, Abe Mitchell, Billy

Burke, Al Espinosa, Johnny Farrell, Morrison, Davies, Bill Mehlhorn, Joe Turnesa, the Dutras and at least eight or ten more. Quite a different job!

A truly great shot, I suppose by definition, has to be for *something*, preferably for all the marbles, something BIG. It has to count—*this* to win the Open. The circumstances surrounding it must appreciably up the ante, adding to the difficulty and throat constriction. It has to be daring, or at least be notoriously, infamously, potentially disastrous that if it doesn't come off it will sear its place in the memory, an accident that one can't help but peek through the fingers to watch while passing.

Another unsung and forgotten but outstanding shot—perhaps effort is a better description—does not meet these high standards but it was among the most courageous and entertaining one could ever witness, and I felt privileged to have seen it.

It went like this: Notah Begay's drive on the Road Hole during the first round of the Open at St. Andrews in 2000 was long and left, diving into the rough separating the 17th fairway from the second. One. His explosion wedge barely advanced the ball from a clump of thick grass. Two. He made solid contact with his next attempt with a nine-iron but it again sailed off target, again left and long. Not just left but so far left that it landed in the famed Swilcan Burn. Three. The famous hazard is in play off the first tee. Only a foozled drive would find it driving the home hole. No one in living memory could recall anyone hitting into it playing the infamous 17th, golf's most notorious par four. But that's where Begay's ball came to rest.

It was unfortunate for several reasons; most of all because through the preceding 16 holes his play had been stellar. It was only the first round but he'd been on fire, and this was, after all, golf's oldest championship. He played the front nine in 31 strokes (five under par) and pushed the pedal to the metal to an exceptional eight-under par.

Those unfamiliar with the burn (a small channel wide enough to

CHURCHMAN'S CIGARETTES.

GENE SARAZEN.

tempt the inebriated to jump across it) can appreciate that it is not a pretty sight up close, awash with the usual flotsam and jetsam of litter and muck, pulled by the ebb and flow of the tide, and washed to the nearby sea. One must be careful in passing judgment. British professional Max Faulkner once had the audacity to refer to Carnoustie's Barry Burn as a sewer. He was immediately upbraided. "Don't you call that a sewer," a lady overhearing the remark chided him. "That's the Barry Burn, and there have been a lot of gowfers as good as you in it afore the day."

The tide was out for Notah, luckily, but the ball was still partially submerged if remotely playable. Begay, like Sarazen, took little time making up his mind, if only because the longer he surveyed it, the worse the prospect of something positive happening would've appeared. He tucked in his trousers and hopped down in, successfully hoisting the ball back into play. The shot caused a sensation. Full-page photos graced the back covers of the next day's tabloids. Like Sarazen's "one for the books," the shot was notable at the time but went down in the other book, the one that matters—the ledger—as a disheartening triple-bogey seven. The earlier good undone the sterling round was tarnished. He limped home with a bogey. His swan of a 64 transformed into an ugly duckling of a 69, still a very good start, but his run at the title had sustained a body blow. He finished a very respectable tied for seventh, though thirteen shots behind his buddy, Tiger. Notah parred the Road Hole each of the next three days. As pros will if they are to survive, the PGA Tour's first native American took the experience in stride.

"It is something I will always remember," he said after the round. "It was a lot more interesting than taking a boring drop." That it was, if expensive.

Once, perusing the Decisions Book, the weighty but absorbing addendum to the Rules of Golf, I was reminded of Sarazen's predicament. My guide with respect to the rules was always the late Bill Penn, executive director of the Texas Golf Association. Bill could make the rules interesting to a layman audience, no small undertaking. One didn't have to be an attorney, which Bill was, to understand them, he said, but it didn't hurt. Henry Longhurst took them to task for decades in the hope that an applicable set could be made to fit inside a matchbook. Other than not blowing one's nose on someone's backswing, he wrote that the rules were "mostly nonsense," a curmudgeonly view that persists alongside their growing complexity and a cottage industry that seeks to translate them to the masses. In these litigious times, consideration now is given to such things as crawfish mounds, molehills and dead land crabs.

Out of bounds, where to take a drop, these may induce quizzical looks even among those expert officials who will earnestly confide that if "you haven't blown a rule, you haven't *done* rules." That's how hard they are to interpret.

Rule 24-2b/15 is one of the few that can be recited without hesitation from memory, although I don't suppose it would've helped Sarazen as things turned out in the hot dog stand. Knowing "Opening Barn Doors to Play Shot Through Barn" may not make you your group's "rules guru" but, as is printed on a Manhattan cab receipt, it "can't hurt, could help."

> Q. May a player open the doors of a barn to enable him to play a shot through the barn?
> A: At the risk of getting shot, as long as no eggs are broken, and goats are not involved in any way, why the heck not!

No, no, that's not it. Just kidding. This is the actual answer:

> A: Yes. A barn is an immovable obstruction, but the
> doors are movable and may be opened.

Thinking about that rule, the various circumstances involving the farmer, the golfer and, likely some aggrieved barnyard animals never fails to lighten the load. A toast, then! To The Squire and the enterprising Native American, and to those brave if barn-swallowed. May we all live so long as to have the occasion of successfully invoking Rule 24-2B/15; to pull off the shot, when desperate times call for desperate measures with the inspired brass of Sarazen and Begay, even if in the end it lands on the card as a miserable seven, or we lose the hole. Slainte!

• • • • g l o r i o u s
u n c e r t a i n t y • • • •

With broken nerve and swollen head,
I woo the sleep I cannot wed,
And view again, with ceaseless dread,
    That stymie.

In vain I seek relief with curse,
A big, big D, or even worse;
To that I owe my lighter purse,
    That stymie!

I've suffered much from fortune's knocks,
But sorrow's crown, a ball that blocks,
And hideous squats and grinning mocks,
    A stymie!
        —Golf Illustrated, 1902

the stymie

It left golf with barely a whimper but what a bang the stymie packed. Its origins are something of a mystery. It likely came in around the mid-eighteenth century if not before. Early permutations of the rules reference the *stimy*, but note it a word of imprecise origin. We do know that efforts to rescind it date back *at least* to the 1830s. Apropos of a litany of criticism and controversy, it would not go without a struggle. Differences of opinion were duly noted in the preface to the 1952 uniform code. Unable to reach any consensus on several alternative proposals, the bell finally tolled. "Abolition of the stymie was therefore recommended and adopted." That was it. A centuries-old tradition was officially excised from golf.

A connoisseur's shot, the stymie really only pertained to those better players who competed and played strictly by the rules, then as now a minority. It left at an interesting time. The advent of television, a go-go post-war economy, and an unrepentant golfer in the White House spurred a national golf boom smoothing the way for pro golf's ascent. Years before, however, the stymie presented official golf with a spiritual fork in the road.

Even those traditionalists who in the end favored abolishing the rule lamented the change. "Golf is a game that is full of breaks," wrote USGA President John J. Jackson in 1934. "If breaks are in our favor we like them; if they are against us we ought to accept them,—and a stymie is one of the breaks."

It was an enlightened if increasingly old fashioned view. A more palatable opposing outlook was expressed in an old caddie yarn. In *Golf Architecture*, Alister MacKenzie mentions the old Scotch major who when he clears it, the stream is a "bonnie wee burn." On the days when his ball finds a wattery grave, it's "that domned sewer." That was how those opposed to it saw the stymie, a source, as one critic alleged, of "peculiar viciousness."

Evidence of the depth of feeling the stymie engendered, even its most eloquent and last great advocate couldn't stem the tide. Bob Jones was dead set against its elimination. Charges of unfairness were unwarranted, he wrote in *Golf is My Game*. They "can have gained acceptance

only because the victims and their sympathizers have felt justified in ago-
nizing over their tragedies." In other words Sore losers!

Golfers, of course, are still very much like that, martyrs to the end.
The ancient tug between how things were back in the good ole days and
how they should be, of course, still wages. Those who nostalgically
favored the stymie feared the unattractive consequence of distilling
chance from golf, which—coincidentally—remains very much on the
minds of traditionalists. Those who care and consider luck an essential
element of golf mourn pervasive homogenization. A course may look
good on television. It may produce low scores and be groomed to yield
uniformly good conditions, lies and bounces. Whining may be kept to a
minimum, but it wearies some who watch the PGA Tour and prize old
fashioned artistry over power and precision. Again, this is a familiar
lament, with each passing generation nostalgic for the past.

Thirty years before the shot's repeal, at a speech at the Drake Hotel
in Chicago in 1922, another USGA President, Howard Whitney,
warned against what he viewed as "a growing tendency in the country
among players to make the game easier and waive penalties." That effort,
continually reprised on behalf of more easily integrating new players into
the game, continues today at regular odds with the stewards of golf. The
stymie's demise may have been inevitable. It may have been a genuine
improvement, for the rules continue to evolve in the game's perceived
best interests, tugged and prodded by technology, whim, common sense
and good intention. Doing away with the stymie may have leveled the
competitive field of match play, and, as many thought, was long overdue.
Its demise ultimately belongs on that list of debatable—and, yes, sadly—
uniquely American double-edged "innovations:" the golf car, more exact
course markings, fivesomes, lush, environmentally unsound conditions,
gated communities, and satellite range-finders. Even the dominance of
the more impersonal stroke play format over the rigors and satisfactions
of match play is evidence of our influence, traits more suited and prefer-

able to the American character. Richard Tufts sussed the American dis-
taste for the stymie back in 1936:

> Americans are perhaps a little over keen to win and are
> not sufficiently content to play the game for the game's
> sake. They grow impatient and condemn any element of
> luck that breaks against them and it is just possible that
> their opinion of the stymie rule might vary somewhat as
> it breaks for or against them.

For traditionalists of an earlier era who prized self-sufficiency, who
preferred colorful names rather than numbers for their clubs, who cherished unpredictability, doing away with the stymie was a triumph of
change over charm. Whether golf is a better game without it is a question only those who experienced first-hand its "glorious uncertainty" can
adequately answer. Whitney's adroit remark back in 1922 will be true as
long as something called golf is played in an organized, collective fashion: "I believe," he said, "that what we have today in the game is the best
that has survived."

Iin many an important match the stymie struck the decisive blow.
Bob Jones arguably owes the Grand Slam to a deftly-played stymie in the
1930 British Amateur. Another great stymie-assisted win occurred in
Walter Travis's historic 1904 British Amateur run. Whether by design or
happenstance, in the days before balls could be marked on the green, the
stymie permitted one ball to block the other. To negotiate it, required
ingenuity and skill—and luck. One ball could be played over another, or
bent around. Pulling it off courted disaster, most unfortunately, by
knocking an opponent's ball in the hole. This happened countless times
as it did memorably to Johnny Farrell in his 1931 Ryder Cup singles
match with Bill Davies.

Hard to imagine there was a time, way back in the 1700s, when an
opponent's ball was fair game, similar to croquet. "Provided the player

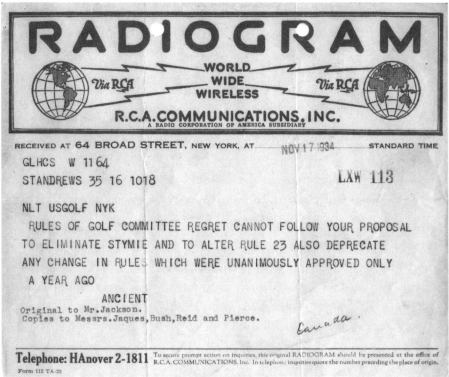

A difference of opinion regarding the stymie crossed not only generations but for a long time, the Atlantic.

does not touch the adversary's ball with his club"—this from the 1814 code of the Edinburgh Burgess Golfers—"it shall be deemed fair to play a ball against the adversary's ball." Only when balls touched or were within six inches of each other could the closer ball be lifted, a vestige of the Leith code in 1775. Eventually it was decreed that if balls came to rest six inches or more apart, the stymie was in play. If the balls were closer than that, the front ball could be lifted.

We have a good example of the ruckus created by the stymie from 1807. The Scottish *Weekly Statesman* that year reported that the "harmony" of the Royal Burgess Society had been "seriously disturbed" over an incident when it appeared Francis Braidwood [a golfing name if ever there was one] had removed his opponent's ball "when it was lying in a direct line between him and the hole." The Leith rules allowed for this, others then in vogue did not. "The dispute developed so acutely that the Society was split in two," reads the account. The schism lasted nearly two years before the two sides buried the hatchet. Minutes relating to the affair were ordered destroyed "to obliterate all record of this unfortunate affair." Another six years passed before the gold medal competition resumed.

The most impassioned and articulate U.S. attack on the stymie was penned by William Everett Hicks in a 1909 article for *Harper's Weekly*. In the *Iniquity of the Stymie* Hicks challenged that it "billiardized" the game. He asked good questions. "If a ball is not allowed to intervene with an opponent's ball "through the green," why should it do so on the putting-green?" He had a point. In fact, at the 1931 annual meeting of the California Golf Association this very criticism formed the basis of a resolution calling for the stymie's elimination:

"WHEREAS: One of the outstanding features of the game of golf is that each player shall play his own ball uninfluenced by that of his opponent, and that the spirit of the stymie is unfair and in exact contradiction to this situation…"

Indeed, the stricture of allowing one player to play a ball at rest unimpeded by his opponent was what made golf different from other sports, and, yes, more civilized.

The stymie breached this hallowed rule. It allowed weaker players a unique opportunity to recover. (Deftly played,) A deftly-played stymie could negate the advantage of the golfer who, for instance, hit more greens in regulation but was then thwarted by an opponent who hit less commendable shots through the green. The weaker player could counter-punch from behind with a block. Hicks likened the stymie to a marathon in which over the "last half-mile or one hundred yards [runners] should be allowed to elbow one another or otherwise block one another's progress." The stymie, he argued, opposed the game's very spirit. And why, he wanted to know, have golfers qualify at stroke play for a championship that would be properly contested at match play AND include the scurrilous stymie. There were other charges. Hicks complained about the shot's inherent difficulty. No one on the traditionalist side would buy that, however. "A stymie can be learned with sufficient time and application," defended Jackson: "If he has done this why not reward him over the less diligent player?"

Two years later, in *The Problem of the Stymie*, Hicks again sought to defuse "a long and tedious controversy which might strain the amicable relations between the players of this country and Great Britain." Differences among American golfers regarding the stymie were one thing. There was also the opinion of the game's other rule making body to consider. Up until the end, indifferent to American pressure, the Royal and Ancient Society of St. Andrews remained disinclined to do anything about the stymie. A serious attempt floated by the USGA was shot down in the mid-thirties. A Radiogram and follow-up letter in the USGA's archives dated November 19, 1934 reads:

> Rules of Golf Committee regret cannot follow your proposal to eliminate and to alter Rule 23. Also deprecate any change in Rules which were unanimously approved only a year ago.

Hicks thought he had an amicable solution. With two balls on the green, the player who lies closer to the hole (having hit a better shot) should be granted a stymie *should he need it*. His idea was to restore advantage to the player he believed had rightly earned it. Same for the player who gets to the green in fewer strokes: the stymie would afford the better player from tee to green an ace up his sleeve. Rewarding the better player who, by virtue of his skill, needs no additional recompense circumvented the whole possibility of the stymie. So, not much of a solution at all. No more was heard on the subject from the enterprising Mr. Hicks.

Hicks *was* right about one thing. Say this for the stymie: it offered the lesser player a parachute. Just getting the ball on the green was no assurance that the hole was won. Better golfers, Hicks included, must have been infuriated to see a good drive and a sound approach thwarted by what they construed as a lucky shot. No question it added another layer of pressure and uncertainty on the putting green. That was both its beauty and its… iniquity.

His was but one of many attempts at finding a compromise. In the mid 1930s, the USGA polled amateur golf associations across the country. The October 1937 survey found the split almost down the middle: twenty organizations were in favor of continuing, twenty-six were against the stymie. Bob Jones ironically noted in his assessment of the debate that those against, as they always are, were more vocal than those in support.

Participants in the 1936 Massachusetts Amateur were asked to respond to a series of questions about the stymie. They played without it that year. For example:

- *In your opinion did the elimination of the stymie change the outcome of your match or matches?*
- *In your opinion did it speed up or delay play?*
- *Did you enjoy playing your matches more or less with the stymie eliminated than you would have had the stymie rule been in force?*
- *Did it speed or delay play?*

Not surprisingly, the comments from Mass Am golfers went both ways. T.O. Holcomb of West Roxbury: "In my opinion the elimination of the stymie had a decided influence on the outcome of our match." He thought play was "materially" slowed by the unnecessary marking of balls. He didn't care one way or another but "if the elimination of the stymie has as one of its purposes to speed up play, I am afraid it failed in my eyes this year." Others disagreed, including E.E. Lowery of Charles River: "Without question (elimination) it helped speed up play. Majority believe it did." Gerald Anderson from Worcester insisted: "A match with the stymie eliminated is decidedly more enjoyable."

The debate raged on. H.F. Russell, a Utah rules official, reminded once again that: "You do not improve a game by making it easy." The stymie "is a part of the history and tradition of the game." He likened it to the tip-off in basketball, which of course has over time also been tinkered with. The groundswell against the stymie meanwhile gathered steam. The California Golf Association "moved to this action by popular opinion" again stepped up in advocating its removal.

The USGA Executive Committee responded directly to the repeated California challenges, again emphasizing allegiance to the game's history and tradition. An undated memo closes:

> Perhaps of all games, golf is the least mechanical. The implements with which it is played follow an accepted pattern, designed to emphasize the skill of the player and minimize the mechanical results. The courses on which the game is played are of infinite variety. The thrill of the game would be gone if it were played on standardized and level grounds as is football or tennis. Golf is full of "breaks" and a stymie is one of them. In the long run they even up and they always add to the variety of each match and the pleasure of playing.

As champion committee member Jay Monroe wrote the *Newark Evening News* in January 1936: "...the thrill in golf is not necessarily in having everything perfectly fair and in playing the game with mathematical precision." Monroe confessed his conservative bias. He was just too stubborn to put a sand wedge in his bag. He tried several "and know that my results average much better, but I will not use them since I get more thrill in playing a trap shot with the old niblick." As they say, hard core our Mr. Monroe.

There might be those, as an editorial in the *Chicago Golfer* noted, "who would like to have the cups made larger, the fairways wider and hazards reduced in number. Naturally they oppose the stymie. ...If all sports were reduced to mechanical science and the element of luck eliminated they would lose much of their charm."

Despite these noble forays, at least as early as 1937, alternate drafts of possible revisions to the rule were circulating among USGA officials.

The more I read about the stymie the more intriguing it became. What must've it been like to *lay* one? A 1934 set of cigarette cards led the way to Dai Rees, the great Welsh champion and Ryder Cupper. On card #22 (out of a set of 25), he offers this brief treatise, which may stand as one of the most tersely worded, complicated instructional tips on record:

> ...lets the natural angle of the club-face do the work of lifting the ball when playing a stymie. His stance is with the feet close and almost square, the weight being about evenly distributed, or very slightly over on the left leg. The ball is nearly opposite the right foot and the club-face is laid back. The club (niblick) is taken back with a very slight wrist movement, the left elbow at the same time dropping a little. At the end of the back-swing the club-face is well open. As the wrists move forward the club is pulled through by the left elbow rising. The hands move slightly from right to left and the club-face tends to cut forward and inward across the ball. The very slight shoulder movement is more of a rock than a twist.

One golfer who might capably internalize the difference between a rock and twist is Ben Crenshaw. In an engaging instructional book, based on the discovery of a cache of photos and instructional notes belonging to Bob Jones, Crenshaw tried his hand at laying a stymie, still a source of practice green fun when he was a lad.

His recommendations in *Classic Instruction*:

- Stay down through the shot
- Hit the back of the ball first with a light but crisp, descending blow so as to just clip it off the putting surface.
- Be careful not to take a divot out of the putting surface!

There was talk one year among the Golf Collectors Society that members were going to be allowed to play stymies in the annual "hickory hacker," a tournament played with wood-shafted clubs. More amusing than the rumor was the imagined reaction of the surprised greenkeeper upon hearing the news. One-hundred and twenty period pieces dressed in ties, straw hats and plus fours descending upon his greens, prepared to hack them up with sharpened niblicks—talk about fun! The rumor was, sadly, unfounded. I found myself wondering where I might put Ben and Dai Rees's methods to the test.

There was one last resource to consult. Harvey Penick and Bud Shrake were then completing their second collaboration. Their first, the "Little Red Book" was well on its way to transcending sales figures to rival McDonald's. Bud's stories about the book were almost as much fun as those in it. People came from all over the country and beyond, he said, just appearing on Harvey's doorstep seeking a lesson from the contented oracle. Little did they know that a lesson with Harvey might not last as long as it takes most people to brush their teeth. He was happy to talk with anyone as he truly enjoyed people. No one was refused though they often left unfulfilled scratching their heads trying to decipher "take dead aim" and his other simple teachings. I'd been advised before going over for a visit to write down everything Harvey said, but I got too caught up

in the moment. My notes are eclectic. He said something about swimming being bad for golf; I don't know what we were talking about that
brought that on. He talked about Ky Laffoon, an eccentric Arkansas professional with some Cherokee in him. A successful touring pro when the
money was negligible, Laffoon allegedly once shot his putter and buried
it in the 18th green at Dub's Dread, still a sterling municipal course far
from the sprawl of Orlando. That reminded me of a conversation I once
had with Dick Taylor, the Golf World sage. Who did he think had the
worst temper among the players he'd seen? He offered to think on it.
Hands down, Ky Laffoon, he said later. Laffoon once tried to punch out
a shower head.

Harvey also told me that Lyndon Johnson occasionally came over to
the old Austin Country Club to hit balls. There is a donated Johnson driver on the wall at Burning Tree Country Club but I was skeptical. It was an
incongruous picture. Johnson, a man who looked happiest in the saddle, on
the driving range? Austin Country Club was not fancy—but golf? That
was for Roosevelts and Kennedys. Years later, in the course of some unrelated research, an intriguing bit of evidence surfaced: early in his career
Johnson publicly confirmed his interest in the game. A profile in the 1948
edition of something called *Men of Achievement* includes this nugget:

> The new junior senator from Texas lists his hobbies as
> golf, hunting—and politics.

Johnson was then fresh from winning a notorious senate race over former governor Coke Stevenson, a true Lone Star hard scrapple icon known
as "Mr. Texas." The campaign continues to fascinate Johnson scholars for
its intensity, contrasting styles and voting irregularities. Golf would presumably have been no use to Johnson in attracting votes out in the Texas
hinterlands. Still, there it is. Perhaps he thought it was just the thing junior senators were supposed to do, or that it would've appealed to President
Roosevelt, though stricken with polio but once an enthusiastic golfer.

REPLACE DIVOTS

So what was LBJ's swing like? Harvey just slowly shook his head, a comment-no comment befitting a Washington insider, or—for that matter—a country club pro who knew how to keep secrets.

Another more distant name from the past also came up. Jim Barnes, a dominant force just after the First World War had authored a seminal oversized book of photos. *Picture Analysis of Golf Strokes* went into multiple printings. An okay first edition remains a prized possession, $75 back in the late '80s; no telling what they're going for now. Harvey started talking about having cleaned his clubs and mentioned a photo in the front of the book. What was he talking about? As soon as I got home, I ran to the book shelf. Sure enough, there was a photo of the 1921 U.S. Open champion's ten sticks lined up against a door, specs included. (He used a 42" driver, interesting given the 'Human One-iron" went 6' 4.") The book came out in 1919; but it could've easily been decades since Harvey last laid eyes on a copy. I guess you never forget cleaning a U.S. Open champion's clubs. Oh, that Penick boy was sharp.

Could he teach me how to hit a stymie? He let the question sit for a moment; had he heard me? Then he looked at me archly.

"You don't need to know that," he said.

It was true. The stymie was gone years before I was born. Pressed, Harvey offered to share a stymie-related trick. It didn't work all that well on his carpet but it works like a dream on a practice green. Just make sure the superintendent is looking the other way. The trick is simply to line up two balls next to each other, as if one had stymied the other. Step down slightly on the back ball, pressing it into the ground. Then putt it with a normal stroke. The back ball leapfrogs right over the front ball, pretty as you please. I wished I'd asked Harvey about this sleight of *foot's* derivation. Was it an illegal surreptitious trick of the trade from the days when the stymie served as a great, if maligned, equalizer? I wonder. He probably wouldn't have told me even if it was. The wizened teacher would've likely leaned over and regarded me sharply before telling me, quite rightly: *you don't need to know that.*

• • • • bibliography • • • •

The following is a selection of books drawn upon for this work.

How to Keep Your Temper on the Golf Course by Tommy Bolt with William C. Griffith, David McKay Company, Inc., 1969

This Game of Golf by Henry Cotton, Charles Scribner's Sons, 1948

My Golfing Album by Henry Cotton, Country Life Limited, 1959

Study the Golf Game with Henry Cotton, Country Life Limited, 1964

Play Better Golf by Henry Cotton, David & Charles, 1973

Fourteen Clubs and the Auld Claret Jug by Norman Dabell, Contemporary Books, 2000

The Darrell Survey Equipment Almanac 2004, Darrell Survey Company, 2004

The Rise of Warren G. Harding 1865 – 1920 by Randolph Downes, Ohio State University Press, 1970

The Walter Hagen Story by The Haig, Himself, Simon and Schuster, 1956

Peace is Every Step by Thich Nhat Hanh, Bantam Books, 1992

How You Played the Game by William A. Harper, University of Missouri Press, 1999

Golf in the Making by Ian T. Henderson and David I. Stirk, Henderson and Stirk Ltd., 1982

No Cheering in the Press Box, Recorded and Edited by Jerome Holtzman, Holt, Rinehart and Winston, 1974

Michael Jackson's Complete Guide to Single Malt Scotch, Second Edition, Running Press, 1991

Into the Bear Pit by Mark James with Michael Hardy, Virgin Publishing Ltd., 2000

Wilson Golf History—Catalogs, edited by Jim Kaplan, Second Edition, Vintage Publishing Co., 2000

Discovering Donald Ross by Bradley S. Klein, Sleeping Bear Press, 2001

Golf is My Game by Robert Tyre Jones, Doubleday and Company, Inc., 1960

Following the Leaders by Al Laney, Ailsa Inc., 1991

Bobby Jones and the Quest for the Grand Slam by Catherine M. Lewis, Triumph Books, 2005

Bobby Locke on Golf, Simon and Schuster, 1954

Us Against Them by Robin McMillan, HarperCollins Publishers, 2004

Golf A Turn-of-the-Century Treasury, Edited by Mel Shapiro, Warren Dohn and Leonard Berger, Castle, 1986

Golf Secrets Exposed by Bill Mehlhorn with Bobby Shave. M & S Publishing, 1984

● ● b i b l i o g r a p h y ● ●

In Character by John Mortimer, Penguin Books, 1984

The Harding Era by Robert K. Murray, University of Minnesota Press, 1969

The Greatest Game of All by Jack Nicklaus with Herbert Warren Wind, Simon and Schuster, 1969

My Story by Jack Nicklaus with Ken Bowden, Simon & Schuster, 1997

The Open Championship 2000, Edited by Bev Norwood, Hazelton Publishing Limited, 2000

The Feeling of Greatness by Tim O'Connor, Eyelevel Videos Inc., 1995

All Those Mornings...At the Post, edited by Lynn, Maury and David Povich and George Solomon, PublicAffairs, 2005

Dispatches from the Sporting Life by Mordecai Richler, Vintage Canada Edition, 2003

The Shadow of Blooming Grove by Francis Russell, McGraw Hill, 1968

Thirty Years of Championship Golf by Gene Sarazen with Herbert Warren Wind, Ailsa, Inc., 1987

The Encyclopedia of Golf, edited by Donald Steel and Peter Ryde, The Viking Press Inc., 1975

Reminiscences of the Links by A.W. Tillinghast, Researched, compiled, designed and edited by Richard C. Wolffe, Jr., Robert S. Trebus and Stuart F. Wolffe, Tree Wolf Productions, 1998

How to Play Golf by Harry Vardon, Methuen & Co. Ltd., 1919

The Gist of Golf by Harry Vardon, Rutledge Hill Press, 1999 (1922)

Afternoons with Mr. Hogan by Jody Vasquez, Gotham Books, 2004

The Big Beat by Max Weinberg with Robert Santelli, Contemporary Books Inc., 1984

My Memoir by Edith Bolling Wilson, The Bobbs – Merrill Co., 1939